Endorsements for
Journey Pink by Michelle Viscuse

In her masterful first book, *Journey Pink*, author Michelle Viscuse artfully brings the reader face-to-face with her childhood experiences with the unthinkable. With a unique combination of vulnerability, faith, and grace, Michelle recounts deeply hidden memories while courageously confronting her abuser as an adult. Steadfastly leaning on her faith in the healing power of Jesus, participating in ongoing counseling, and ultimately displaying an unthinkable degree of forgiveness, Michelle's memoir is a source of hope for anyone exposed to the horrors of childhood sexual abuse.

—Brett Blair, Ph.D. Author of From *Autopilot to Authentic*

Journey Pink is a powerful, courageous story of healing from childhood sexual abuse. For others who are suffering and hiding, living in shame and silence, Michelle's story shows that healing is possible. It provides helpful insights into the damage that can be caused by sexual abuse as well as the challenges of healing, but it always points to the reality of restoration and freedom in Christ. I'm sure it will be a great encouragement to anyone on a journey of healing from childhood trauma and those walking alongside them.

—Lesley Crawford, blogger at Life in the Spacious Place and Journey to Heal mentor

Journey Pink is a worthy read filled with resources and encouragement for those who have experienced childhood sexual abuse. Michelle Viscuse takes readers through her journey from abuse to freedom in facing the truth and her abuser in this memoir. This empowering book shows the process of working free through therapy. Gifting others with this book will help those who have been abused with undeserved hurts.

—**Carolyn Knefely,** co-founder of
Christian Communicators conference,
international speaker, Bible Study leader, and
founder of TeaCupLiving ministries.

Dealing with childhood sexual abuse can be tricky and challenging, but if you want to know how to move forward, let Michelle's memoir guide you. With courage, she shares her personal journey of breaking free from childhood sexual abuse and biblically based wisdom to show that hope is possible in the midst of incredible difficulty. This memoir offers practical guidance to help you break free from the secrets of the past and build a brighter future full of love, acceptance, forgiveness, and peace in Jesus. If you desire freedom from the stronghold of past sexual abuse, this memoir is for you. You deserve to experience healing and wholeness, so don't hesitate to gift yourself this life-changing book. Now's the time to reclaim your joy, don't miss it!

—**Dr. Temitope Keku,** Professional Coach,
Speaker, Author of *Weathering Storms:
Finding Treasures in the Ruins*, founder of
Hidden Treasures and Riches Ministry

Michelle's courage to speak what was formerly unspeakable and her faith to follow Jesus despite hard questions make an inspiring, powerful story. *Journey Pink* is rich with truths from the Bible that address beliefs and feelings so common in childhood trauma survivors. Though she shares her pain with candor, the heart of this story is about redemption and the power of Christ to heal what seems impossible. I highly recommend *Journey Pink* for survivors and those who love them!

—Lyneta Smith, author of *Curtain Call*

For the survivor longing to feel seen, loved, and free, *Journey Pink* is a must-read! Michelle has done a beautiful job of sharing her personal experience of finding hope and healing in Jesus Christ. Her compassion for the reader is evident through the pages of this memoir. An inspiring read for teens and adult women alike, who have experienced the ravages of childhood sexual abuse!

—Crystal Sutherland, author of *Journey to Heal: Seven Essential Steps of Recovery for Survivors of Childhood Sexual Abuse* and founder of Journey to Heal Ministries

Through *Journey Pink: The Story of a Princess in Need of a King*, Michelle Viscuse gifts the reader with an honesty that is pure and not shocking, only tenderly surprising. As a woman whose life professionally was to serve children and women in danger, I believe this memoir will only strengthen the importance of those in fields of prevention and protection. Now retired and an artist and writer motivated to create redemptive works, I was moved to tears throughout Michelle's story. Her story of childhood sexual abuse and the bravery to examine the layers of its mark on her life is filled with instances for readers who have been harmed at the brutal hands of others to be shown empathy. This book is an invitation to healing, an invaluable invitation to a deeper relationship with our Savior, Jesus. I pray any woman who has experienced abuse as a child or adult will receive this truthful book.

—Lisa Anne Tindal, Artist, Abuse Survivor and author of *Look at the Birds*

A Memoir of Healing from Childhood Sexual Abuse

Journey
PINK

The Story of a Princess
in Need of a King

MICHELLE VISCUSE

JOURNEY PINK: THE STORY OF A PRINCESS IN NEED OF A KING
Published by: Journey Pink, LLC

ISBN: 979-8-9883239-0-7
Copyright © 2023 by Michelle Viscuse
Cover design and interior formatting by Nelly Murariu at PixBeeDesign.com.

For more information on this book and the author visit: https://journeypink.com

Library of Congress Cataloging-in-Publication Data
Viscuse, Michelle
Journey Pink: The Story of a Princess in Need of a King/Michelle Viscuse 1st ed.

Printed in the United States of America.

Journey Pink is dedicated
to survivors
who long to feel seen,
loved, and free.

CONTENTS

A SPECIAL NOTE FOR MY READERS

I see you.

You are tired and worn out, but you get up every day and keep going. You move in slow motion. Some days feel like a slippery slope, yet you survive. You are thankful to be okay, considering you have spent too much time worrying about everything that could go wrong. You live and breathe what-ifs that tend to keep you up at night. Along with rehearsing what you may have said wrong throughout the day, you try reading the minds of those around you.

You are a stressed, frazzled mess, but you smile anyway. Others envy you because they think it comes easy. They think you have it made. They have no idea. If they only knew the real you.

They don't see inside where it is very lonely, filled with anxiety and panic. Others don't see you shut down and disappear when you are overwhelmed. They aren't aware of the bad dreams that keep you awake at night.

So, you keep smiling and surviving. What else can you do? If you tell someone, they may wonder what is wrong with you. And if you could say something to someone, what would you say to them anyway?

You don't even know what is wrong because it is all you've ever known. You think it is just you. You think it is how God made you.

You feel incredibly flawed. Broken. Less than. You feel like a mess. You work hard, you show up, and you say yes.

You want others to like you, and you do not like to disappoint anyone.

You know a lot of people, but very few—if any—know the real you.

You are not even sure you know the real you.

The real you is hidden. But I see you. I know the real you is in there.

Hoping to be seen.

Wanting to be loved.

Dying to be free.

I see you because I've been there.

Jesus gave me hope, and His hope changed everything.

This is the story of how He saw me, loved me, and set me free.

He will do the same for you, and my prayer is that you will let Him.

Be seen.

Be loved.

Be free.

INTRODUCTION
Spring, 2000

At my first women's conference, the keynote speaker came onstage dressed in all white, and I thought, *Wow, she looks like an angel.* Laughter filled the room as she shared some funny stories, and then it got quiet when she shared some of the bad decisions she had made in her life. My mind drifted to my own bad choices. There were plenty.

Suddenly, alarms went off inside me when she mentioned that someone sexually abused her as a child.

I sat there, stiffly, holding my breath and wondering how she became an angel. And I knew right then that it could never happen with me. The mean voices in my head accused and overturned any sparked hope by screaming that what happened with her would not happen for me. It seemed as if I were stranded on an island, and the helicopter that came to rescue me flew away in the opposite direction.

I could not and would not be rescued.

I could only continue to do what I knew how to do ...

Survive and keep my mouth firmly shut.

My body rested back against his chest as I sat cradled in his lap. My eyes followed his finger across every word he read from my favorite red Childcraft book, Poems and Rhymes. *The poems at the beginning were my favorite, and he would read them over and over until I had them memorized. He would call me smart and tell everyone that I could already read. Then he would hand me the book to prove it. My tiny finger barely touched the page as it danced across each word I said out loud. People were amazed, but in reality, I didn't know how to read. We fooled them every time. Our first little secret.*

Chapter 1

I FEEL GREEN

FALL, 2012

I sank back into the corner of her pillow-filled sofa, hands folded on my long, frumpy skirt. Deanna handed me a clipboard with client intake forms to fill out. With shaky hands and a pounding heart, I flipped through the pages and came across the word *confidential*. My eyes popped wide open with panic. The what-ifs fired in my head. I didn't want anyone to know about me seeing a counselor, and I certainly didn't want them to know why. I kept my head down as tears rolled down my cheeks. I had already crossed a line by stepping into that room, and there would be no turning back now. I had to make sure I could trust her.

I looked up. "Will you ever tell anyone what I say? I don't want *anyone* to know, and I don't want you to call the police or anyone else. You gotta promise me anything I say will stay in this room."

She didn't seem shocked by my request—or my flood of tears. Her eyes locked with mine, and she calmly said, "You are safe. This is a safe place. I want you to be able to say whatever you need to say here."

Without blinking, I leaned forward and whispered, "Promise me you won't call the police. I don't want to get anyone in trouble. I'm scared."

1

She came closer. With a gentle whisper, she reiterated, "You are *safe*, Michelle. It's okay. I'm here to help you."

I held tightly to the signed papers, and we sat there staring at each other in silence. I took a deep breath and sighed out loud as I blurted, "I feel green."

I knew it didn't make any sense, but Deanna, my new counselor, didn't seem puzzled. "Tell me what you mean by green," she said.

"I feel green. May is my birthday, and my birthstone is Emerald. When I say I feel green, I'm not talking about that shiny, brilliant, beautiful green. This green isn't like the dark, rich hues of Christmas or the pretty pastel mint of spring. This is an awful, ugly, disgusting green. In a box of crayons, it would be the broken one with the knotty texture and the frayed paper showing its name for all to see. *Ogre.* The crayon that stays in the box. It hates to be on display, especially when surrounded by brighter, shinier, smoother, and nearly perfect crayons. This crayon hides, and when it does come out, its disgust is magnified."

I took another deep breath, and she remained silent.

"This awful green permeates my entire body from the inside out and makes me feel like something is wrong with me. Like something has always been wrong with me. I've worked all my life to hide it. I never wanted anyone to see it. But recently, a friend at church told me she and some other moms teased about how my husband and I were Mr. and Mrs. Perfect. While she talked, I smiled and held my breath as my brain screamed, *I'm not okay!*"

Deanna nodded for me to continue.

"She made me realize I've always pretended to be okay. That my life is fine. But I have always been far from okay. I'm falling apart. I keep having bad dreams, and all these awful memories keep popping up. I feel bad and guilty all the time. I look confident, but inside I see myself as a burden to others. I believe people only tolerate me. This neon ogre green is awful. I know you can't see it. But it's there. I feel it all over me. And it's exhausting. Most of all, I'm tired of pretending. I'm not even sure I can anymore."

I shared how I'd been going to Zumba® four times a week and started losing weight. I loved the movement and the loud, pounding beat of the music, but things inside of me were being shaken awake, especially in my mind. Memories and horrible secrets I packed down long ago were bubbling up. I told her I wore a lot of pink to remind me that I'm not green.

Deanna glanced at my pink nail polish, watch, and pocketbook and nodded. "We'll work through this together and take it slow."

I quickly replied, "Recently, I brought a small hoodie towel into the bathroom. As I wrapped it around my daughter's tiny body, I had a flashback. Images rushed to my mind, and my heart pounded wildly as my entire body froze. It only lasted seconds, but it took me back to being a little girl again. That awful green. Please help me. I need to get through this as fast as possible. But I don't even know where to start."

Random information continued to flow from my quivering lips. "I went through a small box of mine from the attic, which caused me to remember even more. The things in that box uncovered much that I buried in the deepest parts of me. There were letters from friends and my high school memory book. A few friends described me as *wild*. It all pointed to a me that I have a hard time thinking about. It makes my stomach hurt. Looking through the box embarrassed me. Shamed me. One small box. But this all seems like a giant box. A pitch-dark basement full of filing cabinets. Some of the drawers are open. Other drawers are locked up with no key. The folders are out, and there are lots of pictures strewn everywhere. The smells are awful."

Deanna loved the box analogy and used it to help me see that I could bring it with me each week. We would open it and sort through it together. "Once we're finished, you can leave it all in the box. It can wait until our next session. You are free to do other things, and you don't have to stay inside that box 24/7. It's not going anywhere. We will eventually get through it. I know you want this to be over as soon as possible, but the pace is very important. All of this can feel like trying to drink water from a fire hose. We need to get you to a place where you can taste the water when you drink it."

"Yes, it feels like a lot of water is coming out all at once. Sometimes I get so overwhelmed. It's like I leave. I check out or something. I'm there physically, and I may nod my head, but I'm gone. Long gone."

It seemed weird saying that, but again, Deanna understood. She said something about containment and boundary work. She made a square with her arms and called it "the window." Then she said, "Our goal is to get to the window enough to do the work but not too much to overwhelm you. You are free to speak up at any time and define the window. You can always let me know when it's too much or if you want to go deeper. I'll also check in with you and try to keep us in the window."

Tears were still sliding over my cheeks when she said, "Cry as much as you want. You are free to cry. Crying is necessary because this is grief. But you are safe. Crying is welcomed here."

Fifty-five minutes flew by. I couldn't believe it. Hard? Yes, but I liked Deanna. And I did feel safe. I went to the front desk on my way out and made an appointment for the following week.

That night I stood at the stove cooking pasta with my head down while I discreetly wiped away tears. My youngest child ran through the kitchen with his airplane and stopped to hug my legs. As he took off, he announced, "Mommy is sad again."

At church that Sunday, we all sat together on the second pew on the right. I like being up front because it helps me focus. As we stood to sing, my quivering lips hardly made a sound, but the second row helped to hide my face and tears.

After church, we all went for a hike. The air refreshed me. Being alone with my husband and kids in the middle of the woods made me—at least for a moment—forget the wrong in my world. When we stopped to take a break by the rushing waters, the kids climbed on the big rocks. Their laughter made me smile. In these precious moments, my life became peaceful and serene. Innocent even. I grabbed my phone to capture it and begged, "Smile. Look at Mommy." *Click. Click. Click.* My heart longed for these images.

THE VOICES

In my next session with Deanna, I told her I wondered if I were crazy and gave her the example that I heard all these mean voices in my head.

"What do they say to you?" she asked.

I spit them out with ease. "Who do you think you are? No one likes you. No one wants to spend time with you. You are a burden to others. You are fat. You are a bad mom. You are merely tolerated."

She called it negative self-talk and encouraged me to think about where those lies came from, then focus on the truth.

We talked about fear. I confessed how I worry about everything. Always concerned that something terrible is going to happen. "Maybe I left a candle burning. Did I leave the door unlocked? What if we get into an accident? Did I set the alarm? What if someone breaks in and kills us?"

Again, she had a name for this. She called it doomsday thinking. It gave me a little relief saying what went on in my head. It helped even more to hear she had words to describe those thoughts, and that I'm not the only one who has them.

"I've always heard mean voices and worried too much. I've always had dreams, but lately they've been absolute night terrors." I whispered, "Sometimes I wake up in a panic because it seems so real. It takes me a few minutes to sort out the dream versus reality. I don't even want to sleep, but I tried something this week that helped me. Please don't think I'm an alcoholic. I stopped at the store, bought two beers, and drank them right before bed. I've also taken Tylenol PM, but that makes it hard for me to get up in the morning."

Again, she did not act shocked. She assured me she didn't see me as an alcoholic and that we would work on self-care and learn new ways to cope. She asked me what I usually did before bedtime.

"I love to read. Right now I'm reading *The Wounded Heart* by Dan Allender. The only time I can read it is late at night because the cover says, *Hope for adult victims of childhood sexual abuse.* So it's not like I can carry it around. I wish he'd named it *Tangerine* or something else. It terrified me to order it online. Thankfully, a dear friend knew my wish and brought it to me in a paper bag. I've been devouring every page."

"Tell me what you like about it," Deanna said.

"In one part of the book, he describes the devastating effects of childhood sexual abuse. When I read the description of the party girl, it struck a nerve. I mouthed *wow* because it helped me understand my wild self and some of my actions. I want to reread it. It's helped me so much, and I wish I had read it sooner. I felt so alone my entire life. So singled out. Now I know the truth. Others have experienced this too. Not only me.

At the end of our session, I told her about a seminar I attended with a friend whose husband had an affair. The speaker used a powerful illustration and said the day of discovery is when the line is drawn in the sand. It's where your life now becomes two parts, the before and the after. It reminded me of the part in Allender's book where he references the girl who looked at two pictures of herself as a child. In one photo she looked happy (before abuse). In the other picture, she looked hollow and vacant (after abuse).

As I stepped out the door, I turned to Deanna and said, "I can't see my line. I don't remember a time before the abuse."

Later that night, I woke up startled from a dream. I saw myself in a small casket at a funeral. Unrecognizable. A blob in a tiny, white, square box. When people walked up to look inside, I screamed, "I'm in here. It's me. I'm alive. Help me!" No one heard me or even recognized me. I wanted them to see me and help me, but no one acknowledged my screams. They all glanced inside, then kept walking. Their expression never changed. I laid flat in the bottom of that box, wishing I could escape, but it seemed impossible. As people continued to look, some faces that appeared made me panic. Other faces made me smile and brought me peace.

When I woke up, I thought of the verses in Psalm 139:13-14, "You created my inmost being. You knit me together in my mother's womb. I praise you because I am fearfully and wonderfully made; your works are wonderful, I know that full well" (NIV).

When I thought of the promise of that verse, so many questions flooded my mind. *Have I ever believed it? Could I believe it?* I knew it to be His truth, and I did believe, but did I know it full well? I had no idea how to reconcile being fearfully and wonderfully made, even knowing that His works are wonderful. I've often wondered why He even made me. *Did He create me to be abused? Is that all I am? All I'm made for?* I wrestled with these questions, but they helped me see I wanted to believe His truth for myself, full well. I didn't recognize my younger self in the dream, but I thought it might be the little girl in me. I wanted to face the pain and anguish to get her out. I needed her to see herself as pink, not green.

I continued to wear pink as a constant reminder to myself that God did not make me green. I had to be reminded because I could feel shame crawl over my skin. The shame became a powerful force to be reckoned with. I focused on all kinds of pink to fight it.

Pink encouraged me to keep going. I started seeing myself and my world in color for the first time. I found myself celebrating my body because it is mine. Pink reminded me that I'm His Princess, and He is my King. One morning I kept hearing the words *Journey Pink*. Then I saw the letters spell it all out for me. P-I-N-K means Princess in Need of a

King. I had embarked on a journey to recognize the princess inside of me and discover the King I so desperately needed.

I thought of the verse in Psalm 34:17-18, "The Lord hears His people when they call to Him for help. He rescues them from all their troubles. The Lord is close to the broken-hearted; He rescues those whose spirits are crushed" (NLT).

The word *rescue* stood out to me. I had always focused on being the only one harmed. I had no idea that what happened to me behind closed doors happened to others. I honestly felt all alone. I envied my only brother, mostly for being a boy. As an only child for five years, my baby pictures were everywhere. I even had my own toy room, but it transformed into his nursery when they brought him home. It didn't seem fair that I had to do things and hide things and carry all these burdens while he enjoyed being a kid and playing with his toys. In all the universe, I thought these bad things only happened to me. Surely they didn't happen to my friends in their homes. I believed I had been singled out. Only me.

When my focus shifted from being the only one harmed, I thanked God for rescuing me. I let the word *rescue* simmer a bit. One minute I felt confident and thankful. The next minute I struggled with the timing and wondered why it happened in the first place.

Right about the time I started counseling, I discovered Susie Larson and her daily blessings. I loved to read them because it seemed she knew all my business. Her words nailed it every single time. I would come across them on Facebook at the right moment. Her blessings gave me hope and encouraged me to keep going.

May God lift you up and heal and restore you fully. May you see glimpses of His glory everywhere you turn. May He show you wonders of His love that overwhelm you and make your knees weak. May He put a new song in your heart and a new dream in your spirit. May you walk forward unafraid and full of faith that your future will be far greater than your past.—Susie Larson

66 You keep track of
all my sorrows.
You have collected all
my tears in your bottle.
You have recorded
each one in your book."

—Psalm 56:8 NIV

Sundays were my favorite. My grandpa would pick me up in his light-blue station wagon and take me to church with him. After Sunday school, I'd stand with my chin resting on the pew in front of me, watching him as he belted, "Oh, victory in Jesus!" His powerful voice made me consider the truth of every word he sang. After church, he would drop me off at home and leave. Mom made lunch, then I'd spend the afternoon in my parents' bed watching TV. My dad would let me watch Shirley Temple. Her curls and spunk made me smile. Years later, I came across Shirley Temple movies on Amazon Prime. My eyes lit up. I had to introduce her to my kids. We all gathered, and as I sang along to "On the Good Ship Lollipop," my skin got clammy. I felt sick. I quit singing and stared at the screen as old images flashed in my mind. I turned the TV off.

Chapter 2

I'M READY TO TELL YOU MY STORY

Dates and numbers have always been significant to me. When my third counseling session landed on September 11, 2012, I decided to tell Deanna everything.

On the way, I missed the exit. Late for the appointment, I went in flustered. She asked me to take a deep breath. I did. We talked a bit about the end of our last session. I admitted I had still been way above the window when I left. This window work of looking back made me feel little and defenseless. Being way above the window scared me. Stuck. I apologized for blurting out how I didn't know when the abuse started. I didn't know how she would figure everything out with me constantly speaking in code.

Deanna let me talk for a minute and then stopped me. "I want you to know what matters is where you are. It's not about me. It's about you. Don't worry about how I may feel or respond, and don't do or say anything for my sake. Concentrate on you. You need to be comfortable. You need to be in the window."

"Well ... I think I'm ready to tell you my story." I stared at the left corner of the room, focusing on the ceiling and then the square. As my eyes zeroed in on the tiny dot where the ceiling met the wall, I went to that out-of-body, safe place and started talking.

I rattled off the bullet points of simple facts in my brain as if I were talking about someone else. My voice sounded monotone and choppy. I wanted to get it all out, figuring we could connect or disconnect the dots later.

- 🔒 "My parents were very young. I wish I had dates and confirmation of when the abuse started, but I don't. I have no memories of it being any other way. I can't remember feeling safe and secure."

- 🔒 "My dad messed with me."

- 🔒 "We started going to a new church. One Sunday, the preacher told a sad story about a family during the invitation. I started crying. The pastor motioned for me to come forward, so I did. My dad followed me. We were baptized together. The abuse continued."

- 🔒 "As a teen, a man over twice my age raped me. I had a mixed drink and passed out. I woke up with him on top of me. After taking a shower, I asked him what happened and begged him not to tell anyone, afraid if anyone knew, they would think of me as a bad girl. I worried any exposure would lead to others discovering the biggest secret in my life. Plus, I had always believed if I ever told what happened at home, I would be the one in trouble, and no one would believe me. The police would take me away. I couldn't tell anyone. Part of me worried since I had been drinking and wearing a mini skirt, maybe that made me somehow at fault. I reasoned there must be something desperately wrong with me to make men do these things to me. If my parents found out, that would expose me even more, so I had to hide this too. Besides, what could they do? The man promised he wouldn't tell anyone. I figured it would happen only one time, but he kept calling and showing up. Now I had more secrets to keep, plus trying to make good grades in school, have boyfriends, and be a typical teenager."

🔒 "Once in college, I managed to get away and see my messed up life. I worked to be able to pay a counselor, but then she left. I graduated, met Anthony, opened my business, met Betty, married Anthony, and all this time, I knew something deeply wrong lived hidden inside of me."

🔒 "Three kids later, as life started to slow down, I started remembering the things I had pushed down so deep. I read the book by Allender and for the first time, a light bulb glowed brightly, shining the truth that I'm not green. So here I am. And even though I know I'm not green, I still question every decision, relationship, and thought because such bad wiring shaped me. And while I can say I'm not green, unbundling those wires seems impossible."

"So there. I did it." I let out a deep sigh.

She smiled and asked, "How do you feel now?"

"Lighter."

Her smile grew bigger. "Yes, because you stepped into the light."

"You're right. Today the darkness is now light. Today, big walls came down in my life. Nothing blew up. I did not get sent to an orphanage. No one died or went to jail. All is well in my world right now because I'm free."

"Michelle, what you shared is horrific and inexcusable, but the fact you shared is beautiful. You may need to shut people out of your life right now. You have to do what makes you feel empowered and in control. If avoiding others or stepping back does that, then it's fine. I want you to only deal with you. Take care of yourself."

Toward the end of the session, I turned to Deanna and said, "Oh, can I tell you there is a tiny part of me somewhere deep that understands they must have had their own issues and that God's grace can cover them like me or anyone else? And I need to forgive?"

She shook her head as she said, "That will come in time. You don't have to go there right now."

"The truth is I'm furious and so upset with them. I'm not sure I can or will ever confront them."

"No one is asking you to do anything. Your healing depends on you. Not them. They can't control that part of you. You can heal and never confront them. If the time comes and you want to confront, then we can walk through it. But that is not your concern. Your only concern right now is *you*."

Oh, the sweet taste of freedom.

As I left, Deanna said, "Michelle, you are going to be fine. Today is huge. Celebrate it. Celebrate the light."

I exhaled deeply, then hurried down the hall and pushed against the door to step into the bright sunshine. I stood there, squinting and smiling as the warmth of the light covered me. I did it. I had a quick Mary Tyler Moore stroll to my car, celebrating my courage. I made it through the hard part. Later that night, I fell asleep happy, but the next day proved tough.

I woke up mentally and emotionally exhausted. So much guilt. The flashbacks were the worst. Memories hit me full force. It were as though a fire hydrant cap suddenly slipped to the side, and unexpected water gushed out and blasted me from head to toe. I would be drenched in shame before I even knew it hit me, all the while continuing my normal daily routine.

At work, an underwriter put me on a brief hold to look for the information I had already emailed. As the elevator music played, I saw myself as a child sitting at a table with a container full of green crayons, furiously coloring. I lost it. When the underwriter came back on the line, she probably thought my tears were about the missing email. She assured me she had what she needed as I tried to calm my nerves.

I don't want my brain to drift there, I told myself. But ... *boom*, it did.

Then a mortgage broker asked me to send over a document. When I emailed it, she immediately replied, "Thanks, Michelle. I love fast people. Have a great day."

Fast? My mind drifted back to the summer before seventh grade at church camp. One of the older boys held my hand and gave me a peck on the lips. I was smitten with him. When we were back home from camp, he mentioned his mom called me *fast* and said he could not like me. I didn't know what it meant. Confused, I asked my mom, "What does *fast* mean ... like if someone says you are fast?" She must've wondered why I asked but never explained. When I finally learned what it meant, I wondered what made his mom say that about me. What did she know?

Boom.

These memories made it hard to focus. After work, I came home and made dinner. I barely ate and soon made my way upstairs to change into pajamas. I curled up on my side of the bed and sobbed into my pillow.

Anthony held me and said, "I'm really sorry and hope this ends for you soon." He gently rubbed my back. A sweet gesture. Still, there I lay ... so alone with these thoughts and memories surfacing.

But as always, Susie Larson's daily blessing met me right on time in the middle of my mess.

> As you wrap up your day, may God grace you with an eternal perspective. Where there's only been disappointment, may you trust God's divine appointment and timing. Where there's been discouragement, may He inspire new courage to stand strong. Where there's been whining and griping, may you find a new song to sing and new reasons for thanksgiving. May He break through the clouds so you'll see just how blessed you are. Sleep well tonight.

I woke up nervous and excited about the Beth Moore Simulcast. A few ladies from my church were attending. I worried about holding it all together in my fragile state.

I didn't.

We sat at a square table. I had my back to them as the tears fell. My shoulders must have shuddered a bit, because at one point, one of my friends patted me on the back and handed me a tissue. At the first break, she said, "Michelle, I'm praying for you. I know you're hurting."

Beth read the theme verse from Psalm 68:11 NET: "The Lord speaks; many, many women spread the good news." What a powerful message. At the end, she challenged us to be courageous and tell our miracle story. My hand ached from taking notes. I kept writing as she encouraged us to overcome our fears and not hide our limps because they make us approachable.

When she said the word *surprise*, I looked up. She stared straight into the camera as I attempted to write down every word.

> All of us love a surprise. We think we don't like the mystery of it, but we do. You can't get control of this thing. He is God, and we can't take control of it. Do you have enough trust in Him to trust Him with the mystery of it? Do you believe He is good? In Him, there is no darkness. God can't mistreat you. God can't fail you. And through it all, He gives us a little something to hold on to. In the mystery, He gives us enough to hold on.

She ended by giving us verses to help overcome our fears. She challenged us to be courageous, tell our miracle story, and let revival begin.

My puffy eyes squinted at the sunshine as we headed to the car. I imagined myself bright green because now others saw me as a wreck. There would be no hiding behind a fake smile anymore.

I sat in the back seat resting my head on the window and staring out. As I tried to dissociate, one of the ladies in the car blurted out part of her story. Then another shared some of the hard parts of her story. My eyes widened as I listened. Eventually, I shared how I had started my own healing journey and had a ways to go. We each revealed some of our struggles. How freeing to take off the all-is-well mask. We continued to talk for a few hours. By the time we pulled into my driveway, I saw myself as pink again and a little bolder.

Then my dear friend Susie came to my rescue again, faithfully reassuring me to keep going.

> May you refuse an anxious heart and embrace a faith-filled one. May you stomp on your fears and dance because of your dreams. May you shun the shame of your youth and hold tight your new identity in Christ. You're not an improved version of your old self. You're something altogether new, profoundly beautiful and abundantly equipped. Walk fully in the blessing and purposes of God today.

66 You, Lord,
are my lamp;
the Lord turns my
darkness into light."

—2 Samuel 22:29 NIV

I found myself in trouble again. My mom told him to spank me. He took me into my bedroom and closed the door behind him. He pulled the black belt off slowly while explaining he didn't want to whip me. Instead, he would pop the belt, and then I could scream so she would think he whipped me. He didn't want to hurt me. Another secret.

Chapter 3

BISCUIT DAY

Arriving a little early for my next appointment, I sat in my car nervously tapping on the steering wheel as the music played. I texted a friend. *It's Thursday. Please pray for me.*

As I walked in the door, the receptionist gave me a wave. I lifted my hand to wave back and wondered if she read the information secretly tucked away in my file. I picked up a magazine and flipped through it. Couldn't read. Didn't want to scroll through my phone. I wanted to get on my safe couch. Finally, my therapist came around the corner. I jumped to my feet.

As soon as she closed the door behind us, I plopped onto the couch and blurted out, "I'm falling apart."

Deanna grabbed my file and sat across from me.

I shared how I dropped every ball I tried to juggle. "Anthony is patient with me, but he's also frustrated. He constantly has to remind me of things. Lately, it's been hard to keep up with our busy schedules. I'll ask him a question, and he'll say we've already had this conversation. He says I don't listen, but truthfully, I don't even remember asking him. It makes me think I'm going nuts because my mind does not slow down."

She nodded. "You're dealing with a lot right now, but it will not always be this way. We can explore ways to help with the additional stress. What else is going on?"

"It's hard for me to shop for groceries and make dinner," I admitted. I don't even want to think about food. I forgot to pay a bill. Luckily, they waived the late fee. And I missed one of the kids' games. Makes me feel horrible. They don't deserve this, and I don't want to be this way. I wish I didn't struggle so much."

She reiterated that it is normal to struggle, especially since I had so much to process.

"I've been thinking about biscuit day so much I've been eating biscuits from Bojangles." My eyes squeezed shut. I shook my head as the memories came flooding back. "I had come home from college that weekend. I lost it with my dad."

Deanna turned slightly in her chair to face me directly. "Biscuit day?"

I glanced toward the left corner of the room. She started writing on her clipboard.

"I stayed out late the night before and woke up with a hangover. My mom came in my room and told me to get up and make my dad breakfast because she had to leave. I got out of bed, shuffled my way to the kitchen, and cracked open an egg on the counter as he came around the corner and asked, 'What's burning?' He pulled open the oven door and plopped the pan of burnt biscuits on the counter. He pointed to the pan and said, 'Look what you've done. You burned the biscuits. They're ruined.'"

"What happened then?" Deanna asked.

"I snapped. Completely lost it. My whole body filled with rage, and I started screaming at the top of my lungs the three words that were forbidden in our home— 'I hate you! You can make your own breakfast. I'm not your slave, and I'm not your whore. I'm so messed up because of you.' I threw in a few choice words I don't care to repeat."

24

Deanna continued to write.

"My eyes twitched. I had never acted or talked that way to him. He leaned against the refrigerator and crossed his arms. He tried to calm me down and said very slowly and sarcastically, 'Well, if I could change things, I would.'"

"And then?"

"I went even crazier, yelling and cursing louder, shaking and pointing at him. 'I hate you! I hate your guts. You have ruined me. I'm so messed up because of you.'"

"And his reaction?"

"He no longer tried to calm me. At this point, he got angry. His eyes turned completely dark. He reached for his belt, so I ran. I took off to my room and tried locking the door, but he pushed it open with his black belt in hand. He whipped my legs and back as I lay face down across the bed, scream-ing awful things at him. With each strike, I refused to cry. Eventually, I stopped yelling and stared at the wall. When I got quiet, he walked out. Once he left, I cried and stayed in my room most of the day until my mom called me to eat dinner. At the table, we all sat there as if nothing happened. We never talked about it again. It almost seemed as though it never happened. But it did. And something changed that day. He never touched me again."

I glanced back to Deanna. She didn't write anything down.

My body felt the rage and the blows as I described the events to her. She helped me come back inside the window. She helped me get grounded by engaging my senses. She handed me a smooth rock to hold and toss from one hand to the other one. I described the vanilla scent from the candle burning on the wooden table in the corner. We both listened intently to hear a small child faintly crying outside the window. I looked back at her and took a big sip of my Diet Coke.

"Wow. You were furious, weren't you?"

"Yes, but this became an out-of-control rage. I said terrible words, even f-bombs. Maybe beyond furious."

She asked me to give my anger a number from one to ten.

I confessed it as clearly a high ten. "I've never been that angry or acted like that before or since."

She looked me in the eyes and said, "Your ten would be close to God's degree of anger. That is how angry He would be."

I had to let her words sink in for a moment. I didn't know how God felt about any of this, but I never thought about Him being angry. I compartmentalized it, thinking God must be okay with it since He said for us to obey our parents. *How could He be angry if this is who He created me to be?* As this truth continued to sink in, I wondered if some of God's anger could be directed toward me. Could God be upset with me? Or maybe His anger stemmed from what happened to me like Deanna mentioned.

We talked about how it felt for the abuse to finally stop. Empowering, yet I still took on the responsibility like everything had been my fault. I remained out of control with my life decisions, questioning everything. It had messed me and my thinking up for so long, and that part didn't change. The only thing that changed? He stopped putting his hands on me. His eyes still probed, but at least he stopped touching me. While carefully applying eyeliner in the bathroom mirror, I would see his reflection in the doorway, watching me.

"I didn't know for sure he would stop touching me after that day. I still walked on eggshells around him and avoided him. But after a while, I understood it had truly stopped. I wish it would've stopped sooner, but I could never say anything to anyone. No way. Too much at risk. Plus, I learned a long time ago if you speak up, even if you are believed, no one will do anything, at least not in my world."

"Why is that?"

"I listened to a child three years older than me describe to adults what happened to her and how the man had a gun. She cried when telling them what he made her do, and she never wanted to be around him again. They brushed her long hair as they lied and told her everything would be fine and she would never have to be around him again."

Deanna nodded.

"One time another child a few years younger than me described in graphic detail what someone did to her in the front seat of a truck. The adults told her to stop saying those things. It didn't end for her either. I learned to hold it together early on and keep it all inside because no safe place existed to tell anyone. I learned to minimize my circumstances by constantly reminding myself it could be so much worse."

"And now?"

"Now, everything is unraveling. I keep dropping hints to Anthony, but can't see what good it would do to tell him. Too many what-ifs. It might destroy us."

Deanna asked me to consider bringing Anthony in for a session. For my homework, she instructed me to focus entirely on self-care. She encouraged me to slow down. "Be in the moment and be present. Feed yourself spiritually. Make sure you eat. Make sure you sleep. Go for a walk with the kids and enjoy it as never before. Enjoy your life. Reclaim the lost joy by enjoying those moments. Laugh. Laugh as hard as you can."

As easy as all that sounded, it seemed impossible. At night I would hit the pillow with a deep sigh. Sometimes I fell asleep right away, but usually I would wake up throughout the night. Once awake, I found it hard to fall back asleep. I would lie there in the dark on full alert, watching the clock and waiting for the first light to peek at me between the blinds.

My vivid dreams were intensely real. In one, I emailed a written copy of my story to one person and told her I wanted to share my story to protect others. When she replied, she copied everyone by mistake, so my secrets were out there. I could not recall the email. I kept reading it over and over. No specifics, and no names. The words were mostly in code, so I thought it would be fine, but it still made me nervous. Then when I went home, a representative for our security system said we needed to upgrade because people could see through our walls and even our clothes. Anthony didn't find it necessary, but I convinced him to purchase the upgrade because I didn't want people to see me naked. I woke up in an absolute panic over the exposure. For several minutes, I fretted over the email and others' X-ray vision into my life. I took a deep breath, thinking, *Only a dream, Michelle. Not real.* But my heart continued to race.

I shook it off and went to work in large-and-in-charge mode. I wrote myself a note to be sure to tell Deanna: *This is the first day in a long time that I feel remotely normal or back to whatever normal is. With a clear and focused brain, I accomplished a lot. I still need to buy groceries and balance my checkbook, but everything else is well in my world. I'm incredibly thankful for this peak. This day of no tears, no fear, no worries, no anticipation. A normal day. May many more follow because today is precious.*

I'm glad I wrote it down because I would have doubted I truly felt that way by my next session. Things were tense in my marriage. Anthony seemed confused and didn't understand. I decided telling him would only make it worse, so I wrote myself a note to remind me never to tell him.

Dear Michelle,

If you ever again contemplate letting him in ... don't.
You can't trust him.
Reread as needed.
Trying to protect you,

That Voice

No wonder Anthony stayed confused. When he asked me point-blank questions, I lied or said something to throw him off. Where before I had been the queen of multi-tasking, I started to forget things. He would get frustrated and tell me I needed balance. In addition to working and being a wife and mom, I now went to Zumba® four times a week, wearing pink and playing Latin music nonstop.

He simply didn't know what to make of me.

One night he texted me to stop at the store on my way home. I forgot and drove right by. When I walked in, he shook his head and walked out the door to go himself. This is why I thought I could never tell him. He would be upset and blame me for everything. Would he throw it all in my face for the rest of my life? When something terrible happened, would he make it about me and my problems? I didn't consider it wise to tell him. Safer to leave things as is. Too much at risk.

And I didn't want the exposure.

HOW BIG IS GOD?

Deanna kept small, smooth stones in a bowl by the couch. They were helpful with grounding. She said holding a stone and tossing it gently back and forth would help me stay in the present. I bought my very own heart-shaped, smooth rock with the word *Hope* on it. As I sat there squeezing the rock, I told her about my dreams and Anthony's frustrations.

Deanna saw right through me and called me on it. She explained that Anthony wanted me to share with him, but I constantly looked for something to prove he could not be trusted. She challenged me to think about how I have patterns of testing people to determine if I can trust them.

"I'm scared he will be upset with me and blame me."

She encouraged me to let my faith and beliefs help me decide what to tell him. "Michelle, it's a matter of trust. It all boils down to how big you think God really is."

"With everything else, God is huge. But with this ... I got this."

She continued to encourage me. "Pray and trust Him. Let Him open the door so you can step into the light of freedom with Anthony and out of the darkness of lies. Be prepared for the human response. It may feel as if you are being rejected when it's really the awful circumstances he's rejecting. It may be hard for you to see the difference. It's not going to be easy, but your husband needs to know. This doesn't mean you have to buy the T-shirt or wear it on your forehead for the entire world to see. But for the one God joined you with, you are not truly joined. Anthony needs to know. It will take time, but it will be worth it. Pray about it. God will prepare him. Right now, you have him so frustrated he can't help but be angry. Have you considered sometimes you may even set him up to disappoint you?" She paused to let me think.

I nodded.

She ended our session by saying, "Do you really believe God is big and He can do it?"

As I nodded again, she leaned toward me and said, "Let Him."

Afterward, I bravely asked Anthony what I could say to help him understand why I needed therapy.

He shrugged. "No, it's okay. Talk to the counselor. She'll have better answers than me. We can coexist until you get through this."

My lies were wearing him out, and his response made me realize I didn't want to be alone on this journey. I decided to let him know by slipping a note into his backpack for his upcoming hiking trip in the mountains. In the note, I detailed how my journey reminded me of climbing a steep mountain all by myself and trying to get to the top. There were cuts and bruises along the way with no one there to help bandage them or keep me warm on the cold nights. The path had the most amazing flowers, streams, waterfalls, and rainbows, but there were also bad storms. It seemed scary to be alone when the thunder boomed and the rain poured. When I finally made it to the top of the mountain, it would be amazing to see into heaven and behold the beauty and bright light of God's majesty. Sure, he could meet me at the top in a parachute with full safety gear and put his arm around me and say, "How are you?" and I could reply, "I'm fine, you?"

Or he could climb with me.

I desperately wanted him to climb with me so we could experience it all together instead of being by myself. All alone.

I called my progress small victories and learned to recognize healthy from inappropriate. Learning how to say no and establish boundaries became part of the process. I practiced saying what I wanted or needed. I attempted honesty in my world filled with lies. Letting the tears fall freely and enjoying the sweet release of crying, I became aware that I internalized things that were not mine to own, and that I should not worry and stress over the mistakes and decisions of others. I could only own my actions. While some of the mountain climb would be alone, there were parts of personal growth and change to share with my husband. I needed him to climb with me.

As I tried to fall asleep later that night, my mind raced with the possibilities. How would I tell him? How much should I tell him? Even though I knew it would be better for him to know, it still felt risky. What if he left me? I wrestled with my thoughts and the sheets until I finally settled down and fell asleep, only to have the dream that changed everything.

In this dream, I walked into the house after work and opened the fridge to start making dinner. I could hear the boys playing video games. The youngest ran into the kitchen and hugged me. A few minutes later, Anthony walked in and asked about dinner. I stopped slicing the peppers and asked him about our daughter. "Is she working on her homework?"

"Oh no, she's not here. She left a while ago. Your dad came by to pick her up and take her to the bridge. He wanted her to wear the new pajamas he bought her."

I dropped the knife in the sink and stared out the kitchen window, feeling faint. Pausing to take a deep breath, I turned and asked him, "Why did you let her go to the bridge with him?"

He put a piece of pepper in his mouth and smiled around it. "What? She finished her homework. She wanted to see the bridge."

I walked back and forth to each room, trying to stay busy and distract myself, worried to death about her. I peered between the blinds again and again. Darkness had settled outside, and my thoughts were getting dark as well. Finally, lights danced across the wall as gravel crunched in the driveway.

My baby girl.

As soon as she walked in, I ran to her and got on my knees to hug her. I held on to her shoulders and stared into her eyes, looking for any signs. I whispered in her ear, "Are you okay? Did anything happen?"

She looked away and started to answer me, but I woke up.

I sat straight up in bed, almost ready to run to her, when I realized it had been another night terror. Anthony slept peacefully, completely unaware of the war waging on my side of the bed. Part of me wanted to wake him and tell him everything. But then I decided it may not be a good idea to start this conversation at 2 a.m.

I did get up and peek into my daughter's room. She nearly smiled as she slept peacefully with her Blabla doll tucked carefully under her chin. Now I became even more convinced I had to tell him. He had to know—the sooner, the better. *But should I tell him before or after his trip?*

And then, Susie Larson got all up in my business again with this blessing:

> May you step out of the hurriedness of the day and step into a pace that allows for a face-to-face conversation with those you love. May you tighten

your belt of truth and let go of the lie that says you carry your burden alone. May you set your face like flint and trust God's promise to carry and establish you. And may you enjoy deep healing sleep tonight. Your Redeemer is strong.

" Great is our Lord and mighty in power; his understanding has no limit."

—Psalm 147:5 NIV

"You are so pretty. Look what you do to me." My stuffed animals were piled high on my yellow canopy bed, watching us as he watched me. I held my shirt up for him, worried someone would come in and see us. Hurry up! my head screamed. I wanted it to be over. I wanted it to be done. Finally, his eyes rolled back, and as they closed, I pushed my shirt back down over my husky jeans.

Chapter 4

NO

My life had been forever altered, and there would be no turning back. I watched old videos and looked at pictures of myself as a little girl. I had compassion for her one minute and hated her the next. She appeared complicated. Too complicated. I had packed her and all the memories away long ago. Unpacking her now seemed disruptive. Almost explosive.

In one of the old videos, I saw myself eating banana pudding at a family gathering. As my tongue licked the whipped cream, my dad quickly panned the camera away to something else. I watched it again. In those few seconds, I could taste the shame. She disgusted me. I turned it off and wondered if feeling green would ever truly go away.

My life had become a lie. My body remained on full alert, and my emotions danced all over the place. Everything intensified. Amped up. I had always struggled with fear, but now it almost paralyzed me. I would get out of bed at three a.m. and drive to work to make sure I hadn't left a candle burning. *Did I leave the door unlocked? Did I turn the stove off? Did I set the alarm?* I worried nonstop about protecting my kids, afraid to let them out of my sight. I didn't want them to play because I feared they would get hurt. But not on my watch. *No, let's not ride your bike today. No, you can't go to your friend's house. No park today.*

Fearful and nauseous, no one around me knew what went on inside. The world continued to spin. Life went on as if nothing had changed. I went to work, paid bills, and made dinner while my life spiraled down a tunnel that seemed to get deeper and darker. I'd always been able to smile and laugh, but now tears fell in front of my kids. I could not explain why. Whenever we saw my dad, I tried to manage everything and watch my kids like a hawk, but could I do that forever?

My life was completely out of control and would never be the same.

In my next session with Deanna, I saw the need to separate from my dad. "I have to protect my kids. I thought I could always control their environment. But I'm not so sure anymore. What if something happens to them? What if he does something to them?"

She let me sit with that thought for a minute.

I brushed a tear from my cheek. "I worry about them all the time. My anxiety is on overload because I'm determined to keep them safe. There are too many what-ifs, and it's all on me.

Her eyebrows raised as she asked, "Why is it all on you?"

I paused then whispered, "Because I'm the only one who knows there is a problem."

Again, silence.

The thought of telling anyone caused my body to physically shake on the inside. Keeping the secret for so many years kept my family together. We weren't perfect, but telling these secrets would destroy us. Everyone thought I had it made. They considered me the *lucky* one. *Would anyone even believe me? Would he deny it and call me delusional? Would the police get involved? Would he kill himself or maybe kill me?* The voices in my head continued to shout those questions to remind me that silence ensured safety. I wanted to scream, but I sat there staring out the window.

I looked back at Deanna. She smiled and assured me we had time to work through everything together. She said she would help me. I believed her.

Every Thursday I drove thirty minutes to get to my counseling session. I went out of town because I did not want anyone to see me. On the way, I would listen to music, pray, and get myself pumped up to share. One Thursday, Deanna had to leave unexpectedly, so when I arrived ready to talk, they told me I needed to reschedule our session. A punch in the gut. Betrayed. Did this make me insignificant? This hour had become my weekly lifeline, and I cried all the way back to work. How would I ever make it another week?

At our next appointment, I shared how it devastated me to miss our session. The loss of expected support triggered old trust issues. She helped me process my emotions and assured me of safety and support. It had indeed been an emergency that caused her to leave quickly. It had nothing to do with me.

My entire being felt raw and exposed, especially as I engaged more. I became sensitive when relating to others. I questioned their motives and sometimes their comments and actions. Conversations replayed repeatedly in my mind and made me wonder what I may have said wrong or misinterpreted. *Did I offend them?* It always seemed easier to stay back and not connect. Connecting more with others gave my brain more opportunities to analyze and doubt.

Recently, in a group of ladies, someone said, "Michelle, you never say no." I told Deanna it came as a simple comment, but it attacked my core. It bothered me so much that I physically backed my chair away from the circle of conversation and shut down.

As the group continued to talk, this thought kept going through my mind: *saying no implies I have a choice.* It rang true. I truly had a hard time saying no. I didn't always want to sign up, help, donate, or volunteer, but when asked, the question backed me into a corner. For me, saying no came across as awkward and almost impossible.

If I couldn't say no at home, how could I say no anywhere else?

Their conversation continued as my mind drifted to all the times I lay there numb and frozen, waiting for it to end.

I never said no. The word did not exist in my vocabulary.

My emotions bounced around like a pinball. In the past, if someone said something offensive to me, I would ignore it, smile, and try not to worry about it. I wore a mask. My heart stayed enclosed in armor. Sticks and stones might break me, but words never hurt me. The dialogue in my head made me tough. I kept all those sarcastic responses to myself.

But now I started peeling back the mask. It took courage to show up for the meeting, and when the woman said, "You never say no," it shut me down and made me regret showing up. I wanted to have friends, but being busy and avoiding going deep with anyone seemed easier. Relationships were very tricky. I wanted to be present and truly listen, but with so much noise in my head, sometimes I would shut down, mentally leave, and imagine myself elsewhere. I could willingly dissociate. When coping became impossible, my mind exited stage left. Bye-bye.

Deanna helped me see the word *no* as a hot button. "Everything feels so intense because you are a microcosm of emotion with everything all packed in and jumbled together. What you are feeling is normal. Others feel that way too, but you are experiencing it for the first time. It's all new for you." She challenged me to consider how I could channel it for good. She believed God wanted to show me how to be sensitive to the feelings and lives of others because we never know what they are going through.

I knew how it felt to offend others and be offended, so how could I be sensitive to it in the future? She shared another example of how I could be open and make an impact without ever having to tell my story.

I told her about the dream I had the night before. "In the dream, I stood in a field near Anthony. Someone else's husband came up behind me and put his arms around my waist. He kept saying, 'I need this. I need this.' I tried to pull his arms off and scream *NO*, but no sound would come out. My struggle threw us both to the ground. The noise caused Anthony to turn around and see me on top of this man. I woke up in a panic because it seemed so real."

Deanna nodded her understanding.

"When I finally fell back asleep, I had another dream about driving. My dad stood on the side of the road waving to me. I tried to avoid him and act like I didn't see him, but he kept calling me. He wanted me to meet with some people so they could sell me something. I didn't want to go, or listen, or buy what they were selling. I went and listened anyway, but I didn't buy anything."

"What do you think the dreams meant?"

"Both dreams made me realize how hard it is for me to say no. In the first dream, I tried my best to scream it, but no sound would come. I had no voice. In the second dream, I wanted to avoid my dad, but he remained persistent. I didn't want to go, but went anyway. In both dreams, I knew what I wanted but had a hard time saying no. It simply wouldn't come out of my mouth."

Deanna explained that although the word no did not roll off my tongue easily, I could now add it to my vocabulary and practice using it.

"It may be hard to say no at first," I said hesitantly, "but with God's help, I can do it."

"Let's go back to the meeting with the ladies. When you backed out of the circle, do you think God would want you to continue to be outside of the circle?"

I shrugged. "Much safer to be outside where I could pull back and not be at risk. At least there I knew what to expect. And while I had little joy, I had little pain. It didn't hurt as much."

"Where do you think God would want you to be? Think about how, over time, the pain will be less intense. Think about what an impact you could make in that circle. Remember, you never have to tell your story. It's up to you. If you do decide to tell your story, remember their reactions may not make you feel good."

"I'm afraid to meet with them again, much less tell them my story."

"Your story is yours to tell. You don't have to share it with them, but I truly feel you need to share it with Anthony. Can I pray with you before you go for you to have the opportunity and courage to tell him?"

42

She stood with me at the door and prayed for me.

On the way home, I listened to two songs about healing. At first, strength and determination filled me. Then halfway into the second one, sadness overtook me. I cried because I didn't understand why it had to be this way. *How could God allow the abuse and all the pain and suffering that comes with it? How could my dad choose to harm me over and over and act as if we were fine? How could he not be sorry?* Those questions rolled through my mind as the tears rolled down my cheeks.

The night before my next session while watching VH1, the video for "Janie's Got a Gun" came on. I sang along.

Anthony looked at me and said, "You know this song is about a dad who sexually abused his daughter, right?"

What? I missed it. How did I know the words to that song and forget what it meant? Or did I miss it on purpose? Either way, panic set in. Would Anthony figure it out? So far, when he asked pointed questions, I lied. That's all I knew to do.

Deanna and I scheduled a longer session lasting three hours. I told her things were better, but exhausting. Flashbacks, triggers, and nightmares were happening more frequently. I would suddenly see images and feel the memory in my skin. All the green shame poured over me like warm glue.

I shared with her about seeing pornography and being watched and touched at a very young age. I didn't have sex until age twelve. She grabbed a big white notepad so we could work together on a timeline. I did the talking while she used color-coded markers. Anything in red meant my husband knew about it. Green meant he had no idea.

A lot of green covered the timeline. Even with all the red I realized he didn't know a lot because I didn't always speak

h clearly enough. I talked in circles and in code.
cornered, I flat out lied.

"Think about what you will tell him. How will you say it?"
I stared at Deanna as she made notes.

"For now, stick to the facts while we are still working on emotions and belief systems," she said.

"I'm so afraid to tell him," I admitted. "I think he'll be livid. I'm not sure how he'll respond or what he'll do, plus I don't want to dump this pain on him. Mostly, I don't want him to reject me." Then I burst into tears and sobbed.

Deanna handed me a box of tissues.

"I know God's mercy to me is amazing," I said between sobs. "Everything I have and all I am today is by His grace. But why did this have to happen?" I stared at the chart and saw all the ripple effects of the abuse. Heavy sadness squeezed my heart. "I'm not sure I will ever understand any of it."

Deanna had tears in her eyes as well. "Me either. I can't tell you why, but I can tell you this. Who does God love the most?"

"That's a broad question, but I believe it's His Son."

Deanna wrote: GOD ▶ SON ▶ a CROSS ▶ Many new firstborns. Then she erased SON and wrote my name. "When we see the cross, we see purpose."

An excellent visual for me.

I knew God loved me and thought maybe He had a purpose for me. For the first time, I considered He could use me to help other people.

I told Anthony about the chart and the timeline. I explained how we used different colors to show what I hadn't shared with him. I told him it helped me see how I struggle to communicate clearly, and there may be things I thought he knew that he may not know.

He focused on the timeline. "Michelle, when did the timeline start?"

I paused and took in a slow breath. "My earliest memories are around age three."

He got agitated. "You need to tell me everything. You told me about the older man who raped you a long time ago. If you can trust me with that, why can't you trust me with the rest?"

I grabbed his hand and put it over my heart so he could feel my panic.

He put my hand in his and said, "I will love you no matter what. But if this is about someone who could impact us now, then I need to know. Because I don't want our kids around him."

My heart continued to thump in my chest. He had no idea.

I played shortstop in softball. I loved to hear the crack of the ball and watch it fly as I tossed the bat. I especially loved it when the ball soared over the fence. My coach would cheer for me and clap, but if I missed catching a ball, he'd yell at me. It embarrassed and angered me because he never yelled at the other girls. He only yelled at me. At the awards ceremony each year, we would all get a trophy. Most of the time, I would get an extra MVP trophy for the most valuable player. I knew I played my best, but I didn't know if it truly made me valuable. I'd always walk away wondering if I really deserved the MVP trophy or if I got it because the coach happened to be my dad.

Chapter 5

FREEZE

Sleep did not come easily, and my dreams were awful—like watching mini-movies that would jolt me awake in a panic. I would finally fall back asleep, but never went into a deep sleep because my body braced itself for the next nightmare.

The most frequent dream involved being chased on foot in a dark parking deck with no exits, running up and down the stairs looking for a way out. It would be quiet enough to hear myself breathing, and then suddenly there would be a loud noise and lights. My feet continued to run. Waking up, I could not wait to get to the safe confines of therapy.

I told Deanna about my difficulty with sleep and wondered if it would ever be easy again. We were two months in, and I seemed to be struggling even more than before. My nerves were shot about telling Anthony. He always wanted to know *who*. But what would he do if he found out?

Deanna again offered to meet with him, either with or without me. She reiterated how I had confused him a lot. He didn't have a clear picture of the truth. "What would you say to him? How would you tell him? It would help if you were comfortable with what you were going to say. Have you thought of how you would say it?" Then she pulled out the big white flip chart again and grabbed her sharpie. In big letters at the top, she wrote *Stages of Abuse* and listed the words:

- 🔒 Target
- 🔒 Groom
- 🔒 Test—reaction/disarm
- 🔒 Isolation
- 🔒 Actual Abuse

As she talked about each stage, giant brightly lit bulbs shone in my mind. When we discussed *Test*, it got intense. I told her how sometimes the abuse would happen when others were around, and I did nothing.

"Why?"

"What could I do?"

She continued to write more words on the board:

- 🔒 Flight
- 🔒 Fight
- 🔒 Freeze

As we talked about each one, I mainly related to *Freeze*. I still do. Hold my breath. Dissociate. Go numb. Get very still. Deanna explained how Zumba® and body movement helped me to shake up and connect the memories trapped inside my body.

I especially froze when I dissociated, so she helped me with grounding. She explained, "It's crucial to stay present and engaged. Use your five senses. See your surroundings. Hear the noises. Smell the scents. Taste food or gum. Toss something in your hands. Try to notice and be aware of the present when you feel stuck in the past."

"I still feel crazy."

"You are not," Deanna assured me. "Sometimes it will be one of the other Fs. It's not always freeze. This doesn't make you any different from anyone else. You know how you arrive somewhere, and you don't even remember taking the exit? Like you are on autopilot? Well, that happens to everyone. But this is a sophisticated way of coping that allows you to deal with the horror of the abuse. You've learned to freeze because you had to learn to cope."

When my eyes shifted to the left corner of the room, she whispered, "Breathe. Look at me. Tell me what part of your body you are focused on right now."

I lifted my hand to my heart. "My chest."

She shifted in her chair and leaned closer to me. "Why?"

"Because it's tight." I could barely get the words out.

She leaned even closer and asked again. "Why?"

Tears spilled onto my shirt. "If I have to put words to it, my heart is breaking."

I glanced at my watch and apologized because we were twenty minutes over. She let me know she understood, and I did not need to worry. I thanked her and went to the bathroom to gather myself. When I checked out, I mentioned to the receptionist about scheduling another appointment for the following Thursday.

"Deanna wants to see you again on Tuesday instead of waiting until Thursday," she said. "So I've scheduled you for Tuesday at ten a.m. Will that work for you?"

"Tuesday it is."

The rest of the day went by in a blur. Somehow, I made it through work and dinner. I woke up to a new day with a new blessing from Susie:

Start a Day Blessing: May God do a brand NEW thing in and through you. May He break every generational stronghold that keeps you from knowing and experiencing His great love for you. May He move every mountain that blocks your view of Him. May He fill every low place with pools of blessing. And may He restore everything stolen so you can have the life He intended for you from the beginning of time. Your Redeemer is strong and mighty, and He loves you deeply. Live joyfully today!

I loved having normal and productive days, but still wondered if I were truly crazy. Maybe things weren't as bad as I thought. Perhaps I made it all up. I would compare my abuse to others and convince myself it could always be worse.

I imagined myself on a Ferris wheel. One minute I sat on top of the world and could see the beauty all around me. Then I landed at the bottom, watching my feet dangle above the ground and wondering if I would ever make it to the top again. The highs were way up and the lows way down. The in-betweens made my stomach hurt. Sometimes I would get stuck, and it would take forever to move again. It was slow and tedious. At other times I found myself heading in one direction, then I would reverse and be back at the beginning working through it again. *Will life ever stop spinning?* I wondered.

The grief can only be described as awful. When I least expected it, it would overwhelm me and make me think I would burst. No announcement to let others know about my pain. No visitation set up for others to comfort me. No meal trains or casseroles. Me all alone in my pain and trying to manage my day-to-day life despite my big secret.

My body threatened to explode with anxiety. I wanted to keep it all pushed down. *Why now? Why is this happening to me?* Maybe seeing my children in their marvelous splendor made it all rush to the surface when I thought it long gone. *What should I do? Step into the light? Tell everything now when I have held it in for so long?*

Now? To whom? And why?

So many questions. They reminded me of the first time I had my vision checked and found out I needed glasses. Who knew you could clearly see the limbs and leaves on trees? Glasses made them crisp. Now, I saw my life, heart, thoughts, and actions through a completely different lens. Everything involved me and my experiences. Not to be selfish, but I analyzed myself to death. *Oh, so that explains why I did it. Now this makes sense. No wonder I stayed reserved in relationships and had my emotional accounts located in offshore banks.* There were extreme contrasts. Green versus pink. Reality versus perception. Love versus hate. All intense.

I also used a magnifying glass to analyze others. I revisited my interactions through the prism of my reality and how they connected. I inspected everyone in my world—good and bad—and saw them in a new way for the first time. For example, a kindergarten teacher became more than a kindergarten teacher. A soft lap. Someone who held me often. Called me smart. Played with my hair. She loved me. Another teacher scared me, but looking back, maybe she tried to reach out. Perhaps she saw something when she scheduled a parent conference to try to understand my anger and help me. Maybe she cared. Maybe not. But I refused to label her as mean and assume she didn't like me.

Angry and consumed with fear, my world threatened to implode. Lives would be destroyed, and it would be my fault. No going back now because I'm the one who climbed on this Ferris wheel. It would destroy me too because everything I created in my mind to survive would be shattered. Those whom I thought loved me didn't. Everything I tried to hide would be brought to light.

What if everyone thinks it's me and I made it all up?

My emotions bounced like Ping-Pong balls. Seeing a child or hearing a song easily made me cry. The reality of my nightmare overwhelmed me, but I said it aloud. I told the secret I had kept for thirty-nine years.

What am I going to do? What have I done?

Shame engulfed me. Not only shame from the abuse, but also from looking through the magnifying glass at myself and seeing every mistake and bad decision. I thought I had already conquered this, but now I revisited it constantly. I saw my young, broken self trying to cope and manage the pain. Numb. Either way, it painted me green. So much shame.

I had to stop and breathe to intentionally recognize and remind myself, "I'm in control of my life, body, and destiny." Yes, I said it and climbed on the Ferris wheel. "I'm in charge now. No one can make me do anything. No one is going to jail or dying. I do not have to be defined by this. No one can make me do something I don't want to do." I had to protect myself and not let others define my reactions—what I needed to do or where I needed to be. It became my decision for the first time ever, and I could take as long as I needed. Even the rest of my life.

I started from the beginning, watching God show up in everything. I looked for His reactions, forgiveness, understanding, and His constant pursuit of me. I looked in His

Word to see it through my new eyes. Much of what I had been taught reinforced my wrong thinking, so it helped to revisit those verses on obedience and submission and see them in this new light. I had no idea what would come next, but I committed to keep moving. There would be no turning back.

I took steps to tell my husband but still spoke in code without being very direct. At one point, I gave him this long made-up story about a bank robbery. I talked about the person driving the getaway car and then spoke of the person who went into the bank and robbed it. Were they equally guilty? What if the driver had no idea the robber stole the money? Did it make the driver complicit?

I confused him by asking about a bank robber, but in my mind, I wrestled with believing my dad acted alone with no help. My mom lived in the same small house, but I don't think she knew what he did. I had an intense fear of her walking in and seeing the abuse, but it never happened. Maybe she truly had no idea. Anthony couldn't understand why I brought up this scenario, but he offered if the driver knew about the robbery, then that made the driver complicit. How stupid to even talk about it. Why in the world would I tell him now?

The scent of bacon swirled in the air as my mom made breakfast in the kitchen beside us. My brother sat alone in the recliner. I laid on the green leather couch in the living room as we laughed together, watching cartoons. My dad came in, sat on the other end of the couch, and shared the Afghan I had wrapped around me. His foot sneaked its way up the blanket, then his big toe pressed into my underwear right as a huge boulder fell on the Road Runner. I grimaced, but never said a word. I laid there waiting to hear, "Breakfast is ready." Beep. Beep.

Chapter 6

LIGHT

One day my husband asked me point-blank, "Who hurt you?" Then he asked me again. This came after I ignored his question the day before.

I didn't want to lie to him, but how could I answer his question? At this point, he knew someone hurt me, but had no idea who or any details.

I cried so hard I couldn't speak.

He kept asking and started naming people. I stared at him. Finally he said, "This is so wrong. I don't know how you can ever heal if you don't confront him. You *have* to confront him."

I sat there, frozen, tossing a rock from one hand to the other while tears dropped in my lap. We had our appointment coming up with Deanna, and I hoped she could speak to him without me and then with us together. I wanted her to tell him what to expect, how to help me, and how to back off.

As we walked to our car after work, I stopped to drop the mail in the slot. I looked back at Anthony and said, "I have never had control. I have to have control of this. I want to answer your questions, but it's really important for me to decide when, where, and how much to say."

He grabbed my hands in his. "Don't worry. We'll get through this together. I promise everything will be fine. We'll confront it, and you will either get an apology or not."

I let go, got into the car, and closed the door. He made it sound so easy, but I didn't feel convinced. Besides, an apology had always been the least of my worries.

NOVEMBER 19TH, 2012, TEN A.M.

Anthony drove us to the appointment. I sat in the passenger seat, changing the radio station repeatedly. He'd never met Deanna. What would he think of her? What would she think of him? How would this play out? Music filled the car as I thought of everything that could go wrong ... or right.

When we went in, I looked at Deanna, hoping she would tell him everything. As soon as I sat down, I wanted to get up and run out but couldn't move. I finally introduced them.

Deanna shook Anthony's hand and said, "I think it's wonderful for you to be here. I'm so glad you came. What Michelle has to say is hard for her to share, especially with you. She's worried about how you will respond and what you will think. I'm sure you will have questions and thoughts, but listen carefully to her." She turned her attention to me. "Michelle, whenever you are ready ..."

I started wringing my hands. Anthony sat directly across from me, waiting. When I first opened my mouth, nothing came out.

"It's okay," he said. "You can say it."

I sat up straight and lifted my chin. I glanced at Deanna. She nodded. I took a deep breath and blurted it out. "My dad sexually abused me."

Anthony stared straight ahead, his face like stone, as the realization hit that it had been someone very much alive and part of our life. Anger burned in his eyes but also fierce protection. After a few seconds, he blinked and told me everything would be okay. Then he looked at Deanna and asked, "What do we do now?"

Deanna reiterated how it is both brave and hard to talk about sexual abuse. She then explained the extreme difficulty of the work we were doing and how it would take time.

Anthony asked me a few questions, the first being, "When did it start and end?" Then he said, "Does anyone else know?"

As I answered him, he seemed to have his own ah-ha moments, taking it all in and processing it the best he could. He knew I went to my dad when I had questions or needed advice. Anthony saw our interactions and my dad's influence over me. My struggles were evident to him, but now they were being seen in this new light.

Then it hit me. I had wrestled with telling him for months. I had become so worked up about how explosive this moment would be, yet nothing happened the way I pictured it. My husband turned out to be very supportive. Something in his eyes made me think we would be okay.

He put his arm around me as we left. I knew at that moment we were both changed forever. We stepped out onto the parking lot and stood there in the sunshine, the gulf of darkness gone. No longer afraid of being found out by him, the light now shined brightly on me with the lie exposed. Scary, but well worth it. The truth set us both free.

Later that evening, I stood in the grocery store looking at greeting cards when a song called "Just a Little Girl" by Amy Studt played. I made a mental note to look it up when I got home because the lyrics resonated with me. Later, I found the song and watched the video online. Wow. The opening scene shows a girl playing the piano in front of a cross on the wall. It reminded me of when I took piano lessons and pounded the keys in frustration. I liked the video because sometimes I still saw myself as a messed up, angry little girl. As I watched, my heart pounded. The little girl inside of me knocked on my chest, begging to come out. Wide awake now, she had no intention of going back to sleep.

I struggled inwardly. The voices would urge me to be quiet and leave it be. I would hear, *No one will understand or believe you. Let it go.* Then the little girl in me would make enough noise to keep me from giving up.

I tried explaining *green* to Anthony. He thought it meant how I felt, mostly my emotions. I described green to him as an entire belief system based on a huge secret no one else knew or would believe. With it, the green paint of shame, guilt, and worthlessness had covered me from head to toe. My goal in life had always been for no one to see it or find out—even though I saw it in every mirror. He still kept seeing it as emotions and feelings. Finally, I said, "Here is a picture of me as a little girl with bows in my hair. Now, paint me green and let me grow up that way. It's bigger than an emotion or feeling."

I didn't *feel* green. The shame *made* me green.

Anthony left for his hiking trip while I went to church with the kids. On the way there, the doubts crept in. *How will we get through this? Why did I tell him?* Sad, isolated, and alone, I sat through Sunday school with the chatter in my head telling me I shouldn't have burdened him with it in the first place. He really couldn't help me. *What have I done?*

I sat in the sanctuary, filled with anxiety. We sang "Hungry (Falling on My Knees)," and I could barely move my lips. The tears spilled over as I sang. I opened my Bible as if I were the only person in the sanctuary and kept reading Isaiah 54:4-8 over and over:

> Do not be afraid; you will not be put to shame. Do not fear disgrace; you will not be humiliated. You will forget the shame of your youth and remember no more the reproach of your widowhood. For your maker is your husband—the LORD Almighty is His name—the Holy One of Israel is your Redeemer; He is called the God of all the earth. The LORD will call you back as if you were a wife deserted and distressed in spirit—a wife who married young, only to be rejected, says your God. For a brief moment, I abandoned you, but with deep compassion I will bring you back. In a surge of anger, I hid my face from you for a moment, but with everlasting kindness, I will have compassion on you, says the LORD Your Redeemer (NIV).

No one could take this away. Not Anthony. Not even Deanna. Christ is the husband who would redeem me. While I thought it would be helpful for Anthony to know, he would not know how or have the power to make me feel better. I knew I should not expect it. I needed to keep putting one foot in front of the other, trusting my Redeemer to carry and protect me. God spoke directly into my spirit and life as I learned to trust Him.

I started to wonder if any of it could be used for good. I didn't understand the ways of God. What could the mystery of God be when it resembled a horror story? How do you find the mystery of God in terror? These questions nudged my heart gently and tenderly.

I know God is not an abuser or the author of evil. He is the ultimate and supreme being. No matter what happened in my life from the evil, God remains in control. Always.

I didn't understand every why, when, and how, but in some way I knew deep down God never left me. He completely protected and blessed me. My sinful experiences of my own doing, while painful, helped me survive. They also allowed me to relate to and encourage others, knowing full well how much grace He extended to me.

I began to see the mystery of God unfold. Many things were happening where I would relate to, find, or see God in the circumstances. I called them *slivers*. Glimpses of God. Hope. God-winks. Sometimes they were hard and made me cry, but I would look for Him and for the good, and He would tenderly reveal it to my heart.

Could there be purpose in any of this? How would God use it? Maybe my story will help someone else know they are not alone, they are not at fault, and they are loved.

I had no idea where God would lead me, but if one person could be helped—for God's glory—that alone would be big enough for me. I wrote on my blog anonymously as *Pink*, but as much as I wanted to help others, my pride and fear screamed *no way!* I didn't want the label, the attention, or to be defined by sexual abuse in any way. Too taboo. Equal tension existed between me wanting to protect myself and help others. Hopefully, I would get to a place where I could find a way to help without exposing so much.

Tears poured constantly and out of nowhere. Deanna encouraged me to write about my tears and consider helpful responses. She knew writing would help me share my feelings with Anthony. My tears represented years and years of trying to appear happy while not crying in hopes of maintaining happiness. All this time, I thought God had singled me out, didn't love me, allowed my pain, and had not protected me. It gave me a very unhealthy perception of God and love.

I wrote about my tears along with all the random thoughts that plagued me night and day. Writing helped me process my thoughts and communicate better with Anthony.

My innocence ... lost. Stolen. Gone. I knew I didn't cause the abuse, but releasing my guilt made me even more aware of how evil, selfish, and manipulative the abuse had been. Tragic. Heartbreaking. It all looked perfect on the outside. People considered me lucky and told me as much. Focusing on the good kept me alive. But now, sitting with the reality of the abuse, the good in my life became minimized. The horror took center stage ... crushing me.

I saw how much I had to escape to cope. It remained very real. I knew how often I dissociated and checked out. Also, the level of pressure, manipulation, grooming, and silencing I experienced screamed *worthless and unloved.* Like garbage.

Did repeated selfish pleasure really mean more to him than me?

I had constant and intensely real fears. Some logical, others not. Police officers terrified me, even when they stood beside me in line at the coffee shop. I imagined sudden doom could happen at any moment. Once fear entered my mind, it multiplied. I could not get it to stop. I experienced loneliness. I had many friends and knew many people, but my five closest friends barely knew me.

I hardly knew me.

I anticipated disappointment to meet me at every turn, expecting to be harmed, hurt, misled, lied to, abandoned, forgotten, ignored, and hated. My mind would play the tape before it happened, so when and if it happened, it hurt less because I already saw it coming. Always angst. Mostly, completely unloved.

How could I be loved and abused at the same time?

Crying helped. The tears were a sweet release. Sometimes I put words to them, but mostly they whispered to me. Crying did not come easy, but my tears were long overdue and needed space.

As I shared some of this with Anthony, I gave him ideas for ways to respond whenever I seemed sad. I suggested he ask if I wanted to talk or tell him anything. If I decided to share, he should listen and let me talk. In other words, *don't try to fix it.* I explained that when I'm processing something—and not looking to solve it—it helps to have him hold my hand or put his arm around me. Any type of positive acknowledgment helped, and his gentle touch always gave me support and encouragement.

I also shared things that were not helpful. I said, "Please don't say things like, *What now? What happened? Why are you upset? Geez!* Those comments make me feel defensive and shut the emotions down. I know you don't like to see me cry, but I need to feel the emotions I have blocked for so long. As hard as it is for you to see me cry, it's hard for me to cry as well, especially if I'm not alone. Even more so if I'm in public."

When Deanna and I met later in the week, we talked about my tears and my talks with Anthony. I shared how he had come alongside me and supported me. She wanted to talk about identity. I had a list of awful labels for myself. The words *ugly, weak,* and *needy* came to mind. As I called them out, we replaced them with new names. I confessed my struggle to see the little girl inside me as *cherished, pure,* and *loved.* She had been locked away for a long time. Now, with the door cracked open, a little bit of light made its way inside. In truth, I wanted to slam the door on her again. At times, the very thought of her repulsed me, making me wary. But she seemed to be getting tougher and determined to come out.

As our family Christmas gathering approached, I confessed my nervousness in seeing my dad. We decided I could physically remove myself by going to the bathroom if the situation became too difficult. Even though scary and uncertain, having a plan and options helped ease my nerves.

Anthony encouraged me to tell the kids and confront my dad, but I simply wanted to get through the day. He knew the whole situation intimidated me, so he reminded me, "You are not labeled. I will stand with you. I'm not ashamed of you." Those words made me stand taller and feel less alone. I had no plans to say anything and hoped Anthony wouldn't either. Talking it through with Deanna helped.

As soon as we arrived for Christmas, I took the food I had prepared inside. When I put it down on the kitchen counter, I could sense my dad standing behind me. I winced when he said, "Wow, I can tell you have lost a lot of weight." The first comment out of his mouth mentioned my body. It made me want to eat a doughnut. Thankfully, I put on my all-is-well mask and made it through the day fine. I even fell asleep sitting up on the couch when we were opening presents and watching the kids model a variety of costumes. I had a lot of time to think on the way home as my brain bounced all over the place.

I spoke my thoughts to Anthony. "Maybe I'm making a bigger deal out of the abuse than it is. I'm not sure why it affected me so badly. But today, I seem to be doing much better. I think I can handle everything now. I managed to be okay in that environment with him." Then I paused and whispered, "Sometimes I wish I hadn't said anything at all."

He almost stopped the car. He turned and looked me in the eye. "This *is* a big deal. I see it as huge. Think about our kids. And no, you are not going to *manage* it the rest of your life. You have managed enough already. I watched today, and it made me sick. Not only is it huge, it's hidden. You have to make people aware of it. I'm not sure what it means for you and them and the timing." Then he shook his head and said it again. "It *is* a big deal."

Anthony didn't always say the right thing, but he got it right this time and said what I needed to hear. Plus, my kids were a huge incentive for me to pursue healing. I cared deeply for them, even when I struggled to care about myself, so any shift to them brought action on my part. And for the first time, Anthony knowing about the abuse would prove helpful and provide a sense of safety. We were experiencing ups and downs, but today balanced out like we were finally on the same page.

It amazed me that when back in an environment with my abuser, I could hold it together and manage fine as if all were well. I could easily pretend. Or so I thought.

A few days later, I fell apart again.

" Fear not;
you will
no longer live
in shame."

—Isaiah 54:4 NLT

I could hear my mom on the phone in the kitchen as he made his way down the hallway to put me to bed. Some nights he'd be in my room for a while. Other nights, a few minutes. He'd lean low and whisper, "Did you catch a feeling?" I didn't really understand what it meant, but I learned over time if I said yes, he'd stop.

Chapter 7

PINK SKY

Anthony and I attended a friend's wedding. As I sat there in the midst of all the beauty and happiness, my mind drifted to thoughts about my own wedding day. My nerves were so rattled. Lots of stress, yet peace. A joyful day sprinkled with sadness. I had mixed emotions at best and remembered thinking, *I wish we had eloped.*

When I entered the sanctuary, my dad stood waiting to walk me down the aisle. I had both hands wrapped tightly around my bouquet. In my nervousness and uneasiness, I did not let go to take his arm. He held on to mine and walked me to the front of the church. As I stood before my soon-to-be husband, I knew I would be transferring a truckload of baggage into our marriage. I wore white but felt far from pure. I smiled in all the pictures but could not wait for it to be over and for us to be alone on our honeymoon.

"You may kiss the bride." I snapped back into reality as the new bride and groom walked past us down the aisle. I stood there with tears in my eyes as I clapped for them. More tears rolled down my cheeks when they announced the bride's dance with her father. Weddings always make me cry.

My dreams kept me restless that night. I woke up early and let my mind race to avoid going back to sleep. As I told Anthony about the dreams, I whispered my biggest fear. "I don't think I can ever confront him. I'm terrified he will kill himself." Then I wondered how Anthony would deal with my fear since his mom died by suicide.

Shocked that I would feel the burden, he said, "Michelle, you are a grown woman. It is not your responsibility. This not a fear you need to have because it is not true."

As we went into church together I said, "Well, I don't think I can do it. I don't think I will ever be able to confront him."

My mind still wrestled with the thought as I went into my Sunday school class. The teacher read the story of the woman with the bleeding issue. She looked at me and asked, "What stands out to you in this story?"

I stared back at her with wide eyes as I gathered my thoughts. "Jesus could have healed her in peace. He could have quietly taken care of everything, but instead, He called her out. She had to share what He did for her in front of everyone."

I sat there, sweating, my heart pounding. I did not want to deal with any of this. At times, I saw no light at the end of the tunnel. Sometimes I wished I had never jumped on the train. At other times, I wanted to jump off. I wished it would take a different track. Anything but living in this ginormous pit of a lie—the lie no longer known and managed by only me. A lie I didn't know how to manage anymore. Living this lie confused and conflicted me.

I didn't know what God wanted me to do, but terror consumed me. And Thursday seemed much too far away.

I rushed into my seventeenth therapy session with Deanna and quickly updated her about everything that happened over Christmas break. "The interactions were much easier than expected. I'm still afraid to confront my dad, but Anthony keeps challenging my fear with truth. My biggest fear is that my dad will kill himself. The reality that he made me so afraid to keep me quiet is heartbreaking. No child should carry the burden of keeping their parent alive by remaining silent. But it's been a deeply rooted fear with a tremendous amount of guilt to go along with it. I'm not sure if my mom ever knew, but I'm hoping she didn't."

I reached for the tissues as Deanna made a few notes. At the end of the session, I told her about a new memory from the third or fourth grade.

"My mom got upset. We were running late to get me to elementary school on time while I walked around in my socks looking for my shoes—again. Looking for my shoes happened almost every morning and so did her being upset. 'I don't wear your shoes. You do,' she would always say."

Deanna nodded.

"I lined up my stuffed animals around the door at night to see if anyone came into my room to hide my shoes. I honestly believed my mom came in to hide them from me so she could fuss at me the next morning. Now, I'm not so sure. I brought it up recently in front of my mom and dad, and the expression on his face when she denied ever hiding my shoes made me wonder. Walking into school all those mornings with tear-stained cheeks ... heartbreaking either way."

Ending the session with sadness, I went back to the office and cried. I found it hard to transition into work mode, especially on Thursdays after therapy. The stress of work made me look forward to Fridays at 5:00 p.m. when I could lock the door and walk away for a bit. I stepped off the sidewalk into the parking lot, my head down. It had been a rough week both at work and in therapy. But when I looked up to see the entire sky covered in pink, it rocked my entire being.

I smiled, thinking God wrote a personal note in the sky directly to me. I couldn't wait to tell Deanna, so I wrote about the experience to bring to our next session.

I wanted to hand her the paper to read, but Deanna said, "Why don't you read it to me? Let me hear you say it. Use your voice."

"Okay. Here goes. My heart believes the pink-sky note from God said, *Dear Michelle, I interrupt your bad day to present to you this important message: I love you. Surely a flowing pink sky will warm your heart, and you will feel me wrap my loving arms around you and assure you that you are complete and whole in me. I'm all you need. This message brought to you by your Father in heaven who adores you.*"

"That's beautiful, Michelle. Keep reading."

"I stopped and thought, *Really, God, for me? Could it really be for me? Does anyone else in the world love pink the way I do for the reasons I do?* I had to take a picture even though there were three cars behind me. I sat with my window down and my phone out, catching it quickly before it disappeared. I rushed home to show my youngest child. 'Come see,' I said. 'God made the sky pink for Mommy' ... but then it disappeared. As quickly as it came, it left. I grabbed my phone to show him the picture, then posted it on Facebook. At first, I only saw my post. Then little by little, other pictures of the same sky were posted."

I paused to take a breath before reading more.

"In some ways, the joy diminished. *Oh, they saw it too,* I thought. Okay, so maybe several needed a pink sky. Whether or not He intended it for me—perhaps it's silly to think He intended it for me—I'm glad I saw it and took the picture. My mood improved 100 percent. Now I could enjoy my weekend, when before, I wanted to crawl in bed and pull the covers over my head."

I glanced up from the paper to see Deanna's smile.

"I started working on the week's lesson in the *Breaking Free* Bible study by Beth Moore. It took nearly three hours to do five days of study. Instead of doing one lesson each day, I preferred to gear up for the climb, take deep breaths, and let out a big sigh when I finished all of them in one sitting. We woke up late for church that morning, and I kept thinking I should rush and get ready. *I need to get to church,* I told myself. *Gotta hurry. Gotta go.* Then God gently asked me, *Why?*"

Deanna gave me that *knowing* look.

"When I honestly looked inside and answered the question, I saw how I focused on my checklist and others' thoughts. I wanted to be good and appear good. But He said, 'It's okay. I'm here with you. Let's have church.' And, boy, did we have some church. That week's lesson discussed "*God's Unfailing Love.*" As I worked through the questions, God and I went to empty places together. I listened to music. I cried. And He continually comforted me, encouraged me, and loved me. When I finished the Bible study, I read an emotional blog post about a lady turning forty who celebrated her birthday by paying it forward. One of the kids came in, and I said in tears, 'Wow, God really loves us. Do you know how much God loves you?' I believe I had a glimpse of it for the very first time."

I took another deep breath and wiped away a few stray tears. "Stay with me, Deanna. This is where it's big."

She nodded.

"Later that week at Bible study, we reviewed all the questions. I sat and listened to others share. Then the leader read the next question, 'Can you think of a time when you were suddenly awash with the magnitude of God's love for you personally?' She looked my way. For once the question prompted me to answer. I looked down at my page where I had written only one word: *hardwoods*. I said, 'Okay, what I have written is in code, and I'm not sharing it. But I will share how I walked out of work on Friday after a terrible week to a beautiful pink sky. I think God put the pink in the sky for me. He made it pink just for me.'"

Deanna smiled.

"As soon as the words came out of my mouth, I thought, *Do you really believe it? They must think you're nuts. Surely, God does not paint a magnificent canvas in His sky for you of all people.* I looked down and stared at the floor. At the end of the night, the leader asked the question, 'How would you explain the difference between God's love and human love, even at its best? Give examples of how God's love differs.' She looked at me again, so I said, 'I'm not sure I answered this correctly, but I wrote, *He never grows tired or weary of me. I do not shock, bore, or frustrate Him. He doesn't turn His back, avoid, or ignore me.*'"

I stopped to take a sip of Diet Coke while Deanna made some notes.

"I don't usually say anything at Bible study. My cheeks were hot. It seemed completely weird to share, and I thought of all the intelligent, practical answers I could have offered. Why did I share those two? They sounded so unsure. So raw.

So real. As I heard the mean voices in my head, the leader turned the lights out, and the video started to play."

I looked at Deanna and waited for her to finish writing. "This is it. Here's the good part. I listened as Beth Moore shared about being drained and worn out from a speaking engagement. She described how the Enemy really attacked her in those moments. She longed for a fresh touch from God. On her way home in the cab she saw a magnificent sunset with beautiful rays shooting down. She mentioned it to her cab driver, but he didn't seem impressed. As they traveled on, she still marveled at the sky from a different angle. They pulled into her subdivision, and she exclaimed, 'I kid you not, that magnificent sunset stood right over my house. God did it for me. He loves me that much. I felt His enormous peace.'"

Deanna leaned forward, listening intently.

"By now my eyes were full, my heart pounding. Every hair on my body stood up. I had chills as Beth continued. 'This is a letter I wrote. It's not biblical, but it's personal about why God loves Beth Moore. It's all of the ways He loves me, and I want to share it with you.' I listened and smiled because many of her responses were quite similar to my own, such as *I do not bore him.* At the very end of the video, as my tears blurred the screen, she looked right at the camera and said, 'Pay it forward.'"

My counselor leaned back in her chair as I finished reading the last paragraph.

"I thought, *Wow, God!* Now, after this experience, this is what I hear: *Attention Michelle, I'm quite capable of painting a magnificent tapestry of pink in the sky for you, and I do love you enough to paint it. While you felt silly sharing what I prompted you to share tonight, I hope you see I'm not ashamed of you. I wanted the ladies in the room to see and know how much I love you. You are big to my heart, and you are important to me. How quickly you doubt, how quickly you forget. How fast you are to deny your worth. So I gave you a roomful of women to affirm and seal in your mind how much I love you and to remind you that you never shock me. You never bore me. I won't turn my back on you. I never have. I made you in My image, and I love you with all of it. With love you will never comprehend, your Father in heaven and on earth."*

I left this session believing God loves me. He really does.

" And may you
have the power
to understand, as all
God's people should,
how wide, how long,
how high, and how
deep his love is."

— Ephesians 3:18 NLT

My favorite elementary teacher lined us all up at the windowsill to trace in the light. As I pressed my pencil against the glass, the boy beside me slid his hand over my pants. I froze. My hand moved over the image in the light, but the rest of my body stayed frozen in fear. How did he know to touch me? What did I do? I didn't know how he knew about me, but I wanted to do everything in my power to keep my teacher from finding out, so I made it a point to be extra good. He would put his hand on my backside in line, and I would meet my teacher's eyes with a smile. I even shared my lunchbox treats with her because I desperately wanted her to like me as much as I liked her. How could she ever like a dirty girl?

Chapter 8

PURE

The pink sky put a smile on my face for a while, but by the time the next Thursday rolled around, I sat in the waiting room holding back tears. I longed to see my counselor come around the corner to call me to my one place of refuge.

Shaking, I finally plopped down on her couch. I said as much as I could handle to make the most of our time together. I told her all about how the pink sky affected me. "I wrote about it on my blog, but it scares me. Most of what I say and write is in code, but it still doesn't seem safe. I think people can see through me, as if they know everything about me. It's terrifying, and I'm not even using my name."

In her usual calm voice, Deanna slowed my thoughts and helped me get centered and focused. "Your body, soul, and spirit are all connected. When your body is harmed, it impacts your soul and spirit too. Think about how the abuse has affected these connections."

"With sexual intimacy," I confessed, "I want it to be pitch dark and quick."

She encouraged me to be more present in my body and suggested keeping the lights on, talking, using candles, and making eye contact with my husband.

We talked about food and its connection to nurture. I recalled a memory from around the fourth grade. "I sat on the bathroom floor with my back against the door as my mom pounded on it, chewing and stuffing the big sandwich in my mouth as fast as I could. She kept telling me to open the door, but I didn't want her to see me eating before dinner. I tried to hide it, but I was always hungry. Even in high school, I packed a lunch plus ate a school lunch. It's never enough for me to eat. I want to be full. I love the feeling of fullness. My relationship with food is not healthy."

Deanna shook her head. "As I said, the body is connected to both soul and spirit. The body is God's temple. What would it look like to take care of it?" She helped me see the toll abuse had taken both spiritually and physically and challenged me to be intentional in practicing self-care.

I offered some thoughts. "I can get more rest and try to eat better. Take walks. Laugh. Get my nails done. Try to be still. I'm starting to understand God is not the *Punisher*. I don't have to tiptoe around Him. I'm thankful for all the ways He protected me. Maybe I'm a miracle."

She agreed. "With the soul, there is a relational piece that needs care. Instead of worrying that everyone can read your mind, I want to help you find your voice and learn to use it. We will practice saying no, and I want you to read the book *Boundaries* by Dr. Henry Cloud and Dr. John Townsend."

It all sounded impossible but good. I wanted to get to a place where I could set boundaries, tell the truth, and be open. Then I said, "Guess what? Lately, my ability to check out isn't working anymore. I don't automatically dissociate. I'm focusing on being fully present and in the moment. Even when I want to leave or try to leave, it doesn't happen like it used to."

She put her pen down and smiled. "It's okay. God gives us everything we need for godliness, and while it helped you survive in the past, you are learning new skills. Maybe you don't need to dissociate as much anymore."

Usually, I let out the big stuff in the last minutes of our sessions. Some call this "doorknob confessions." Sometimes it took that long for me to get up the nerve. At other times, I wanted to avoid saying the hard things. As we were wrapping up, I mentioned an awful flashback at Zumba® earlier in the week.

She reached for her pen.

"We were stretching. I had both my arms raised when the color red-orange flooded my mind. A crushing sensation made it seem as if my ribs were going to pop in half. I struggled to breathe as I rushed out of class and let the cold air from outside snap me back into reality."

Making my way toward the door to leave, I stopped and looked back. "I'll see you next week." I ran down the steps and rushed out into the cold again.

Later that evening after brushing my teeth, I said to my husband, "Wow, sometimes it blows my mind. Like it's surreal. Did you ever in a million years think we would find ourselves going through this?"

"No," he said, "but I'm not surprised because the world is full of evil, and it sucks that it is. It's not fair my wife is not pure."

And that wiped me out.

I went blank.

Anthony frowned. "Why do you do this? What's wrong? You are completely different now. I didn't mean anything bad by it. You are taking it wrong. I meant it in a ..."

Too late. Gone.

He hit a nerve. And while physically still in the room, everything inside me shut down.

I turned the lights off and got into bed, feeling small and insignificant. I lay there in the darkness and closed my eyes. My brain became a pinball machine bouncing from memory to memory. Bright lights and noises would pop my eyes wide open.

A pivotal time for me included changing schools in the middle of the seventh grade. I had kissed two boys from my old school. The first one kissed me at the skating rink. He tasted like grape bubble gum. I kissed the second one. His tongue felt like sandpaper.

When we moved into our new house, we had a snow day. No school. A new friend invited me over to play video games. The two of us were alone because our parents were working. I only stayed there for a few hours, but we ended up having sex in such a short amount of time. *How did I go from bubble gum and sandpaper kisses to sex?* I had no answer, but he gave me his Swatch watch to wear, which made me think I must be special.

I wore the watch on my first day of school with a big smile but soon found out he had given another girl a watch as well. I went into a bathroom stall, took mine off, and slid it into my bookbag. Seeing the watch on the other girl made me think of myself as seconds. Leftovers. And so unworthy. Again.

I stood out as the new student in the middle of the school year. Everyone knew each other and had already made friends. As the new girl, I longed to fit in and be accepted.

As I reflected on those experiences and thought about the innocent but hurtful comment Anthony made, I wanted to scream into the darkness, *no fair!*

I never had a chance. I didn't react to advances. If anyone made a move on me, my response would be to get through it and end it as soon as possible. I always believed I caused it. Maybe I did something to make them lose control. I almost pitied them because I must have made them have those urges. I took on the responsibility, wondering why God made me this way.

Does pure describe me? I asked myself. My answer? *No.*

Feeling less than everyone else haunted me. Not good enough. Always working hard to make people like me. Maybe if I were funny enough or cool enough I would make friends. An intense feeling of responsibility fell on my small shoulders to hide my secrets and pain.

Perspective changes everything. While Anthony truly did not mean for the statement to harm me, the word *pure* triggered me.

I had shared with Deanna how I struggled to believe I could have ever been pure. If so, when? Someone took it away from me, so it made sense for the word to bother me so much—especially as I considered the shame from my own actions. Most of my bad decisions and wild streaks were really about wanting to be worthy. To fit in. To be loved. To numb myself. They didn't make me permanently stained and irresponsible.

Purity and innocence were never possible for me, except maybe as a baby. But I couldn't remember back that far.

Anthony apologized several times. He kept explaining what he had tried to say. He knew how much he upset me and felt horrible. I forgave him and tried to explain how it triggered me. It bothered me how the abuse impacted all areas of my life, old and new.

Triggers became harder to navigate. They were sudden and unexpected and struck with the force of a tsunami. How could a word like *pure* have so much power?

At my next session with Deanna, we talked about some of the small behaviors I used for self-protection and control. On her couch, I sat slumped over with my Diet Coke bottle in front of my face as if it would hide me. Body language is a way of self-protection but also communication.

I spoke in code and overused pronouns to avoid clear communication. I had to feel everyone out and discover the safe things to say. I described events with vague details depending on how others responded. I avoided offending anyone and making them upset with me. Instead of being direct, I tiptoed around to see how my words were being perceived and then gently let them unfold. This gave me the perception of control and allowed me to backtrack if needed. It could be something as simple as, "Are you a Tarheels fan?" My response might be, "I went to Carolina, but my husband loves Duke."

My relationships with others were not deep for fear of letting anyone get too close. If they were too close or knew the real me, they would probably not like me anymore. I always looked for that safe place. *Don't say too much, or you may push them away. Don't be too much.* When I tried to be enough, I would analyze even the minor things I said and worry about making others mad. Going deep with others terrified me and wore me out, so I did my best to stay in the shallow end. Stay under the radar.

I took responsibility for the actions of others. If someone made a bad decision, I thought of all the ways I should have tried to stop them. *Could I have said more? Done more? Maybe I'm to blame.*

I constantly worried about protecting my kids. I wanted to keep them safe. For me, that meant rarely using a babysitter.

Easier to bring them on a date than worry the entire time about what may be happening to them.

Fear always pounced on me and made my insides scream, but no one knew because I wore the I'm-okay-it's-okay-let's-laugh-and-have-fun-because-life-is-good mask. Somehow, dancing that dance made it almost feel true. But in the background, fear always roared behind my smile. And it wore me out.

As a child, the thought of disclosing the abuse kept me frozen in panic. I thought of all the domino effects and assumed complete and absolute responsibility for where, when, and how each domino would fall. For example, if I said, "Dad is abusing me," he might kill himself, making Mom angry and sad. Plus, it would destroy our family. By saying, "Dad is abusing me," he would most likely deny it. The police would come. I would be the one in trouble. They'd send me to an orphanage, and I'd have no family. If I said to the wrong people, "My dad is abusing me," no one would believe me. They would say I'm insane and send me away. All alone. By the time these fatal scenarios played out in my mind, I decided to shut up and smile because otherwise, I'd lose everything.

Even now, the possibilities that could go wrong consumed me from head to toe. All the threats whispered to me in the darkness came to the surface. The lifelong fears and the voices in my head pleaded with me to stop. Too much at risk. Telling *anything* would destroy *everything*.

When I shared this with my counselor, she brought to my attention that God is big enough to handle all the dominos. He is big enough to work things out in each of those individuals and change their hearts.

I knew I could not work it out, but I remained afraid to let Him do it or even believe He could.

In the middle of one sweaty exercise, it hit me. *Everything I do to protect myself and my world leaves very little room for God to do His thing.* Did I really believe He works all things together for good?

Maybe I believed He would work everything out for good if I let go of the fear and trusted Him. My head trusted Him, but my heart had doubts. My head knew about His unfailing love, but my heart had reservations. I wanted to let go of the fear and trust Him with everything, big and small.

I often reminded myself that He is always with me. He will protect me. He is in charge. I don't have to juggle and manage so much if I tap into His strength and follow His direction, leading, and prompting. After holding on so tightly, He helped me want to let go.

I finally decided to let the dominos fall where they may. *He is a big God. I'm His beloved daughter, and I'm simply called to obey and trust Him.* I wanted Him in the driver's seat ... and our next stop would be the basement.

I pumped myself up for my next session with Deanna, determined to go into the basement where I hid my worst memories and deepest hurts.

My youngest woke me up with a kiss on the cheek that morning and told me he loved me "so, so, so much." After breakfast he said, "Mom, come quick. Look at the pink sunrise for you."

I went to his window and snapped a picture of the beautiful pink sky. I left for work smiling, singing, and feeling the love, strength, and confidence I needed.

A few minutes later, someone who lives near my dad posted *Good Morning* with the same pink sky on Facebook.

Another person nearby posted *Great is Thy Faithfulness* with the same image.

The words and images hit me with such an enormous force that I stopped breathing. They sent this message to my heart: *I love you. What you are about to do is going to be hard, but I will be with you. And I want you to understand my love for him is no less.*

Wow. My chest tightened. And there were tears galore. That perspective helped me. I needed to know and somehow understand it.

I cried the whole way to my session. When I went in, Deanna mentioned she would like to record our meeting. I said, "Sure, that's fine, but don't say my name," then added, "but if you seriously want to record, you need to decide if you want to do it today because today, I'm going to try to go into the basement." I told her what happened that morning, and at some point she turned on the recorder.

Then she said, "Okay, so you can see and understand God's love extends to him as well. Where do you want to start today? Did you have something in mind? Last time we were talking about when you moved schools in the seventh grade."

The color red-orange flashed through my mind again. What did the colors represent? Could I name a memory with a color? Did red account for the rage and anger and orange for the main color of the memory?

I sat for a moment and stared at the left corner of the room as my mind opened the basement file. My arms lifted straight up as my dad pulled my mom's silky, bright-orange gown off of me. My chest crushed into a million pieces. I couldn't breathe. His wet mouth seemed to cover most of my face.

I snapped back and stared at Deanna with wide eyes, then told her what I saw.

"Take a deep breath," she instructed. "Relax for a minute. Think back to red-orange. The color's significance. Then find God in the room with you. What do you think? What do you see? Where is God in this?"

I couldn't even imagine God being anywhere nearby. "I don't know how you can put God in there in any way, but if He were there, I imagine He cried."

"Find Him in the room. What is He doing?"

"Mostly allowing me to escape, I guess. To keep me from being smothered and suffocated. I looked to the corner of the room to escape, going somewhere else in my mind and leaving my body behind."

Deanna nodded. "So, looking back, can you see Him with you?"

I assured her I didn't see it then, but by looking back I could see where He protected me a bunch. He provided buffers and safe people, like my kindergarten teacher. She held me, making me feel safe, loved, and cared for with her. She called me a very smart kindergartener.

Kindergarten.

My shoulders hunched as I shrunk back and started sobbing. I needed a safe place even in kindergarten.

"Another deep breath. Let's go back to red-orange again. Where do you see God in the room for your dad?"

"Well, maybe upset. Angry. Disappointed."

"Michelle, how do you celebrate Easter?"

"Um ... what? We go to church and wear black on Friday. Then on Sunday, bright clothes and happy smiles."

"Why black?" she questioned.

"Because Jesus died."

"Why?"

"To save us from our sins."

Deanna leaned forward. "God's Son, Jesus, had His body torn and battered into shreds because of the wrath of God toward sin, to save us and make a way for us. But the same God who loves has wrath that is withheld because of that night on the cross. He has both anger and wrath, grace and love. In that room, wrath. Absolute wrath. He hates sin. But He withholds wrath by His grace and mercy. The same God who allowed you to get that message this morning—the message that, yes, His love abounds even to your dad—also has wrath and anger for sin. He can perfectly balance what we struggle with. He balances anger and grace along with mercy and justice. Can you see His wrath in the room?"

I paused to take in all in. "Yes, but it's hard for me. I get it, but sometimes it's easier to take the blame and responsibility. When I look at my kids, I know I would not want a scratch on them. Even raising my voice with them guilts me. I wake them up in the middle of the night to apologize. To think red-orange for what it is breaks my heart. A child abused. And so much of my life seemed okay. I had a home, clothing, and food. I played sports and took dance and piano lessons. My parents never missed a game or anything. I thought they loved me. The abuse takes away ... everything."

"Good and bad can coexist. No one is perfect. Sometimes even good and heinous can coexist. Good could be there, and it's okay to acknowledge. But heinous is there too."

"I never expected red-orange," I whispered. "Usually, I never had to do that much. I had to be visible with no boundaries. But this was different. I did not willingly participate. I *never* wanted this."

I took a deep breath as I made my way back into the window. Deanna asked if she could pray for me. She asked for permission to stand by me and put her hand on my head. Then she prayed the sweetest prayer of love, wrath, justice, and mercy over me.

I never considered that God would be upset at what happened to me. I always believed Him to be upset with *me*. Deanna's prayer truly touched my heart, and the fact that she asked my permission to stand near me and touch my head stood out to me. It empowered me to know that the boundaries of my body deserved long-overdue respect.

I had moments of sadness and tears throughout the day. There were times when my insides screamed, *Holy cow, this file is too heavy to shut. I don't want to see it anymore. It's too much.* Yet I couldn't quite climb the stairs out of the basement, knowing it would be too hard to come back if I left.

❝ Keep me as the
apple of your eye;
hide me in the shadow
of your wings.❞

—Psalm 17:8 NIV

It delighted me to have my very own red autograph book in the third grade. We passed our books around for each other to sign, but we ran out of time. I brought it home with me. My dad opened it and signed, "You are very mature for your age. Love, Dad." I didn't bring it back to school for more signatures because I didn't want them to see what he wrote about me.

Chapter 9

VALENTINE SPRINKLES

I came across Zechariah 9:9-17 in the Message version of the Bible and highlighted some of the words as they illuminated on the page and in my heart. God affirmed the message of Journey PINK and proclaimed His promises to me. These truths reminded me of His love for me as His princess. I desperately wanted to be free, and these verses anchored me and helped me to keep trusting Him as my King. To keep going. To take the next step.

> Shout and cheer, Daughter...
> Raise your voice, Daughter...
> Your king is coming!
> A good king who makes all things right.
> A humble king ...
> I've had it with war ...
> He will offer peace ...
> I'll release your prisoners from their hopeless cells.
> Come home, hope-filled prisoners!
> This very day I'm declaring a double bonus—
> Everything you lost returned twice-over!
> God of the Angel Armies will protect them—all-out war.

The war to end all wars, no holds barred.
Their God will save the day. He'll rescue them.
They'll become like sheep, gentle and soft.
Or like gemstones in a crown,
Catching all the colors of the sun.
Then how they'll shine! Shimmer! Glow!
The young men robust, the young women lovely!

I had always seen God as a King, a distant ruler. Now I began to see Him as *my* King. An up-close-and-personal King who wanted to give me peace and rescue me from my hopeless cell.

I never thought of myself as a princess. And to be honest, I never cared about princesses. They didn't exist in my world. I couldn't even name a single Disney princess, so I had to intentionally think of myself as one. One day I went to the nail salon and paid nine dollars to have my fingernails painted in bright pink glitter. I stared at the sparkle constantly and reminded myself the journey would be worth it.

Whenever uneasiness wrapped around me, I would look at all the glitter and think, *God, give me courage and strength because I'm weary and want to quit.* It motivated and challenged me to seek God and study His Word. I wanted to memorize His truths and discover His names for me. I knew He had plans for me. And I wanted to trust Him to be my guide.

As it goes with nine-dollar nails, the glitter fades, and the paint wears off over time. The same with life. I would stare at my dull fingers and want to quit—hurt, weary, and disappointed by people and circumstances. There were issues at work, church, and home. All precarious.

But through this series of disappointments, God showed me His faithfulness. While everything around me proved unsteady, He became my rock. He assured me, *These things that are so important and big to you ... keep them in perspective. They can't give you what I'm about to give you. I'm the only gas that will fill your tank.*

I opened His Word to Psalm 119, pulled into His station, and filled up. I'm His. He put His light in me to shine. He whispered to my weary heart, *Rest in Me. Balance. I will tell you where to go and when to step. You are so bent on old patterns it may be hard for you to see at first, but look for them. Be aware before you take one step. Pause. Is it me taking you there, or are you ahead of me? Give it all to me. The heavy darkness that weighed you down has been lifted. Walk to my beat. Slow down and walk in step with me.*

I grabbed a bottle of nail polish and painted my dull, faded nails. The little bit of sparkle brought a smile to my face and reminded me to keep shining.

That night, I dreamt I went into a coffee shop. Everyone had their laptops open. As I waited in line, I saw a screen that looked different from all the others. I couldn't read the words, but there were different colors, fonts, and pictures on the man's screen as he typed—messy, colorful, bright, crooked, swirly, and full of doodling. Beautiful.

Fascinated, I asked him, "How did you get it to do that?"

He pointed to the screen. "It's a new font. You should try it. It's called *Broken*."

Instantly, our eyes connected. I nodded. "Oh, you too?"

Then I woke up.

I had always focused on putting my best "font" forward, but maybe beauty existed in being real. Maybe if I let some of my brokenness show, I would see it in others too and not feel so isolated. Maybe I would find the courage to tell my story.

I had searched months ago, but decided to try again to find blogs like my story. I didn't find much, but I came across a Tumblr account where a girl took pictures of women holding signs of what their abusers said to them. The signs triggered and resonated with me because I heard some of those same statements:

- 🔒 No one will believe you.
- 🔒 You liked it.
- 🔒 Look what you do to me.

I had a hard time reading them but kept clicking. As I scrolled to the bottom, I found the bloggers following this account. I clicked on their blogs and found real stories of true life and despair.

I kept clicking and kept crying. By the time Anthony came home, my eyes and nose were puffy red. I turned into an absolute mess because those stories didn't end well. They were all so sad. Some gave a lot of details and put "trigger warnings" on every post. Tough stuff to take in. Some abruptly stopped posting.

As I tried to fall asleep, the mean voice in my head taunted me. *What are you thinking? Do you really believe your story will end differently? Do you really want to put this out there for all to read? Do you want to be another poster child? This is messed up. Why do you blog anyway? You will be found out, and it will destroy you.* I stared into the darkness as the noise inside raged. Eventually, I fell asleep.

The following day, I walked into my therapy session and said, "My tears start every Thursday." Everything piled up throughout the week. On Thursdays it all poured out through my eyelids. Deanna gently reminded me that self-care needed to be a priority because my body and mind had a lot to process.

I told her about the blogs I read, which reminded me of a dream. I couldn't remember everything about the dream, but I saw a plain pretzel and then another pretzel dipped in white chocolate and covered in sprinkles. In the dream, I kept saying, "Yes, but a pretzel is still a pretzel." When I woke up, I saw the truth. They were both pretzels, but the one with the sprinkles portrayed hope.

"When I read those blogs, I saw plenty of pain, but no hope. I wanted to share my story, but I wanted to share it with hope. Jesus sets me apart and gives me hope in my circumstances. He represents the sprinkles on my pretzel."

Deanna smiled and asked, "Speaking of sprinkles, how is Valentine's Day for you?"

My eyes immediately filled with tears. I looked at the floor. "Hard." I tried to explain but could not put words to it. "I know what it does to me, but I don't know what to say."

"Try."

"I guess it's that I don't want a card, a call, or a post on my Facebook page from my dad about Valentine's Day. I started dreading it last night. So far, he hasn't posted anything. Maybe he won't. Like when he signed my autograph book. So awkward. I wondered what people would read into it?"

"It sounds like you have a voice, and you want to use it. What if you tell him, 'please don't post on my page'?"

"I would probably get emotional. It could turn out to be either good or bad. On biscuit day I used my voice. Things blew up. I'm not sure I want to go there right now. I'm not even sure I can."

She suggested I message or text him.

"That would be better, but then he would know I'm dealing with this."

"Michelle, he already knows what he did. You aren't telling him something he doesn't know. Sometimes you have to say something so God can work in his life. As hard as it is for you to face, it is hard for him to come to terms with it as well. If you say things are going to be different, it may start the process for him and give you your voice. What if he posts on your page today? What are you going to do?"

"I plan to delete it. I could switch everything to close friends only and make everyone close friends except him. Or I could delete my Facebook page completely."

She let me rattle off the possibilities, then paused and stared at me. I didn't blink when she said, "It looks like you're doing what you have done your whole life, thinking of ways to manage your environment. You have a voice. If you don't want him to write on your Facebook page, you can tell him. You can say, 'I'm having a hard time right now, and I don't think it is appropriate for you to write on my page.' Or you can say something you are more comfortable with. Either way, you have a voice. I hear it. *He* needs to hear it."

I agreed, but it would be easier said than done.

Later in the evening, he posted on my page. I wanted to delete the post, but some of my family *liked* it, so I let it stay. I never acknowledged his comment. I wished I were brave enough to call him and say, "Here's the deal ..." but I couldn't.

I don't think I would've brought up Valentine's Day had Deanna not mentioned it. She also mentioned Father's Day might be a struggle, to which I replied, "Actually, the next hard day will be my birthday."

She tilted her head and shifted toward me with her arms on her knees. "Your birthday? Why?"

My birthday has always been the same weekend as Mother's Day. And it's near his birthday. So, it's all entangled, leaving me to swim in the guilt and conflict.

She suggested I think of new traditions for my birthday and new ways to celebrate. "Maybe you should go away. Do something where *you* can enjoy *your* special day."

"Easier said than done."

I didn't have the nerve to call him at this point, but I did change the ringtone on my phone to "Catch My Breath" by Kelly Clarkson. In a small way, it empowered me by letting song lyrics speak for me again.

Anthony helped make my Valentine's Day special by taking me out for dinner. He also gave me a pink candle holder with the word *Believe* on it. I lit a small candle and watched the light dance around the walls and illuminate the word. So beautiful. Believing did not come easy for me. I wanted to believe—believe somehow it would get better and healing would be worth it.

My counselor wanted me to consider how it would feel for the little girl inside of me to be free. She had been locked away in a small, dark closet for so long. Deanna asked, "Do you think we can open the door a bit more to give her a little more space?"

I did not want to talk about what it would require, but she kept going back to it. I finally told her I didn't feel ready to open the cracked door all the way. Once I became strong enough, I planned to swing the door wide open and hold her hand with my head held high. But not now.

"Okay, that is in the future. Maybe we don't have to go straight there today. Let's talk about what you can do now. What small steps you can take today to give her a little more space. How can you get her out of the dark closet with the door barely open? What would it take? Maybe you could adjust your Facebook settings where your dad can't see what you don't want him to see."

We talked about options. She told me to think and pray about what to do. "You can start doing what is best for you and stop worrying about keeping the status quo. Instead of worrying about offending, think about *her* and how long she has been stuffed away in the dark. Think about giving her more space."

A few days later, it happened. I posted some pictures from our Zumba® celebration and became very agitated because I couldn't figure out how to make it where he could not see them or comment. I finally sent him a message on Facebook asking him not to comment on my pictures. Then I abruptly closed my laptop and went to bed. I wanted to get up and do a happy dance, but I lay there pleased with my actions.

The little girl had a bit more space now. Much better.

When I woke up, I checked. The message said *read* but no reply. He didn't comment on any of the photos I posted. This made it a good day to eat biscuits, so I made my way to Bojangles with a smile. Maybe, just maybe, I had more power than I knew.

The cars slowed down. People beeped their horns. The other kids played on the playground as I stood behind the fence with my pants down. I bent over, exposing my bare bottom to everyone driving by. Only three years old and I found it funny—until the preschool teacher came to get me with her ruler in hand. She stood me on the platform facing the playground and bent my hand back before swatting the inside of it with the wooden ruler. Whack! Whack! Whack! She didn't ask any questions. She called my parents, and I sensed big trouble. I heard this story of me mooning the world throughout my childhood. Everyone laughed. It's not funny to me anymore.

Chapter 10

LAVISH LOVE

As I went about my daily routines, I could only think of two words. *I'm angry.* The little girl inside had awakened. Seeing things through her eyes infuriated me. As I thought about what she had to deal with and how she had to hide, rage flooded my veins.

One day when I picked up my kids from school, my daughter said, "Life on the playground is so hard." She went on to describe what happened at school. As she shared her frustrations, I connected with her animated voice and thought of my own playground moments. I thought of the little girl inside me.

Seeing her.

Feeling her.

Knowing her.

Carrying her and all these secrets for so many years.

It all equaled R.A.G.E.

Anger rumbled under the surface. Sometimes interacting with my kids would take me straight to the little girl inside. As they continued to talk about the playground, my mind transported me back to elementary school to the day I stood lined up at the windowsill with my classmates and froze as the boy beside me moved his hand over my pants.

I mentioned the memory to Deanna. She helped me process it by taking me out the window of her office and into the window of my elementary classroom. She knew what to ask and where to take it, then brought me back safely to the soft cushions of her sofa.

My heart broke for the little girl inside me, whom I affectionately started calling LG.

LG thought the boy's actions meant he knew about her. How did he find out? Could people tell by looking at her?

She didn't want anyone to find out. She considered it her fault. She especially didn't want her teacher to know about her flaws, so she made sure to be on her best behavior. She even asked her mom to pack desserts in her lunchbox to share with her teacher to make her smile. The teacher's fire-truck-red lipstick and beautiful smile brought comfort.

I stayed stuck there for a few days with the file open in my mind. Images popped up here and there with floods of memories, both good and bad. I thought of another time from the same year when my classmates and I were excited to release balloons into the air with notes on them. As I turned the corner in the hallway, I saw my dad with his video camera. The surprise shocked me and made my insides jump.

A good memory popped up at Zumba® when we pretended to jump rope during a song. In my elementary PE class, we jumped rope to "Double Dutch Bus." With two ropes going at once, we would jump in and out while singing along. I loved that song. I still do. It makes me smile and tear up. I've always loved the escape of loud music and movement. I knew what it was like to jump between two ropes over and over for a long time.

With a load of shame.
And a heap of pain.
Scared to death.
With a lot of noise.

Loud music and any movement broke the tension away for a bit and allowed calm to carry me—if only briefly.

Along with Zumba®, Sundays were a place of refuge for me. At Sunday school near Valentine's Day, one of the ladies shared about God's love and brought each of us a gift, an assortment of bookmarks made by a local artist. The one she gave me said *Abundance*. It showed an overflowing wheelbarrow with Bible verses in small print. I loved it until I saw the bookmark in the hand of the woman beside me.

Her bookmark said *Hope*. It showed a girl looking in the mirror and not seeing her true self. I loved this bookmark so much I went online and ordered my own set. I even messaged the artist to let her know how much I liked them.

When my set arrived, I saw the *Abundance* bookmark again, right on top. It made me think of the verse in John 10:10 saying Jesus came to give us abundant life. I truly wanted to believe the promise for myself, but I couldn't quite grasp what abundant life meant.

Bible verses confused me. Even when I believed they were true, it didn't mean they were true for me. Some of them made me uncomfortable, especially the verses about submitting, obeying, and honoring your parents.

A few months earlier I had heard a sermon on submitting that really unsettled me. The pastor made a statement that sent me reeling: "For everything she had to endure, I have no doubt she will receive a crown of jewels in heaven."

I stormed out, thinking, *I don't even want the crown!* I could not fully wrap my mind around what he said. I thought it meant my suffering somehow equaled bling in heaven. No, thank you.

Then Sunday came again. We were early, so we stopped to get coffee. As I waited in the car, I reviewed the Bible verses for our lesson. I found myself smiling until I got to the verse about submission again. The statement about the crown of jewels came back to me.

When I looked down to close my Bible, I experienced a tug and a deep whisper in my heart. *You have always had the crown. You were born with it.*

This settled in my heart in a big way. So big that when I walked into class, I wanted to blurt it out to everyone. *Hey, if you don't realize it, you were born with a crown. God made you a princess. You are a princess now, and you've always been a princess.* But I didn't say anything because with all the emotions, I could barely open my mouth.

In the room of seven ladies, the one who had originally given us the bookmarks handed me an 8 X 10 framed picture of *Abundance*. It looked like the bookmark, only bigger and in a gold frame.

"Did you bring this for me to see?" I asked in a timid voice.

She replied very matter-of-factly, "No, I brought it to give to you. The picture is in its original wrapping, and I put it in this gold frame for you."

Amazement and awe would be an understatement. She did it for *me.*

The leader opened in prayer. As she prayed, tears welled up in my eyes. I thought I would explode from the lovefest. We took turns reading the Bible verses for the lesson. When my turn came to read, I had the verse on submission.

I read the verse and could hardly get the last words out as tears fell. I took a big sip of my coffee and choked. I jumped up and ran to the bathroom. I found myself crying and laughing. Laughing because I'd always worried about what people thought of me. I could not imagine what the class thought about me crying and breaking down. Maybe they assumed I had issues with my marriage or submitting.

While perfect did not describe my marriage—and no one could call me the most submissive wife on the planet—this had nothing to do with my marriage or being submissive. The verse triggered me. It made my heart sink and stomach flutter as if I were on an elevator suddenly dropping to the bottom floor.

I found out later why it bothered me so much. During my childhood, my family would sit on the same row in church every Sunday, everything in place. Our clothes and smiles beamed of happiness and no worries. Only as we smiled and listened to the preacher, my dad would open the Bible to Ephesians 5:22 and point to the verse, *Wives, submit yourselves to your own husbands as you do to the Lord* (NIV).

I sat between them, so my mom saw him pointing to the verse. I saw it too. Neither of us said a word. I imagine we both felt the bullet of those words in different ways. For me, guilt, disgust, and, of course, shame. The wife role belonged to my mom, not me. They were married. Husband and wife with me as their child. I sat as a tangled mess between my two parents. And God? Well, I reasoned He must be okay with it.

Someone came into the restroom, snapping me back into reality. I leaned forward to wash my hands and stared at the mirror. I thanked God for pouring His love and truth into my heart. The Lord had taken the very verse that resonated so deeply with my hurt and used it to open my eyes to His truth and crown me with His unfailing love and compassion.

After church, we picked up fast food and went home. As I sat down and glanced over at my daughter, my mouth opened in surprise. A purple crown rested on her beautiful blonde hair. I asked where she got it. She said it came inside of her Happy Meal.

When she saw my inquisitive expression she explained, "Mom, this is a crown."

I grinned and said, "I know, baby. I know." My grin widened when I saw a swan with its own crown at the top of her purple crown.

For the rest of the afternoon, I looked up the verses on the Abundance picture. I wrote them out in my journal and took breaks to rest. Usually, I needed to be busy and accomplishing something. This turned out to be a slow, quiet day. We didn't have them often. In the evening, we gathered for family movie night with popcorn and brownies. Those somewhat normal moments refreshed my bones and spirit. Maybe some of the self-care options Deanna suggested really made a difference and were worth exploring.

I woke up early the next morning with a dull headache. I went to the computer, dashed off a post for the blog, then jumped in the shower. I blasted a song called "Saturate" by Cody Holley and let the water spray over my tears as I sang along. The song literally woke me up a few nights before. I had fallen asleep with the TV on, and the song played loudly in the middle of the night, startling my dreams. I thought a choir surrounded me in my bed and sang to me. I found the song and added it to the healing playlist I kept on repeat.

As I stepped from the shower to turn the music down, I noticed a text from a sweet friend who had moved away several years ago. It said, *Hey, friend, you have been on my mind so much for the past forty-eight hours, so I have been praying for you and your sweet family. I wanted to let you know and see if there is anything in particular I should be praying about with you. I hope you are well. Sending love.*

I typed through tears as I responded. *Oh, sweet, obedient child. I'm sobbing that the God of the universe would prompt you to pray for me and text me. I have been up since 4:30 a.m. God is doing big things in my life right now. It has not been easy. It has been quite painful. But His love is big ... so big.*

I waited for the bubbles to stop to see her reply. *Wow. And how blessed I am that our heavenly Father would use a sinner like me to touch you right when you need it! I sit in awe of how He works. What an incredible tapestry He weaves as He connects our lives.*

I smiled and replied, *I know! Thank you for being obedient to push send. It has changed my whole day and lifted my head two inches higher.*

It has changed my day too. All smiles and I can feel the happy down to my toes. :)

As I continued to get ready for work, I thought of all the times God would bring someone to my mind. Sometimes He prompted me to pray for them, reach out to them, or send them something encouraging. I would pray, but I didn't usually reach out, too worried about what they thought of me. Maybe they'd find my behavior intrusive or nutty. But the text from Melissa gave me a boost of courage to be obedient to encourage others. I certainly couldn't deny it had encouraged me.

With practice, I learned to experience His lavish love by obeying His prompts. I've always been quite reserved and stubborn, uncomfortable putting myself out there by sharing my thoughts and opinions. These promptings often happened in safe places, like my Sunday school class or on my therapist's sofa. The hair on my neck stood up. I had chills from head to toe. The top of my head tingled as I released the words bursting to pour out of me. In these safe places, I found my voice to say some of the hardest things. I looked down at my feet, expecting looks of disgust and rejection, but when I finally glanced up, I saw compassion and the lavish love of Jesus Christ on display.

" See what great
love the Father
has lavished on us, that
we should be called
children of God! And
that is what we are!"

—1 John 3:1-2 NIV

My dad had us all come outside so he could show us his brand-new Sears Craftsman lawnmower. Being the oldest, he wanted to teach me how to use it to mow the yard as one of my chores. I climbed on the cushiony seat. As the sun beamed on my face, I looked straight ahead and kept going. I could hear everyone screaming at me in the background when I drove his shiny silver prize straight into the clothesline pole.

Chapter 11

BOXES

My closet is filled with boxes. Some contain photos that haven't made it into scrapbook albums yet. There are boxes for each child and even a marriage box. These boxes warm my heart and make me smile.

I wanted a box for my journey to remind me it would all be worth it and would get better. The contents were to catalog where I started and how far I've come. Plus, it would be a place where I could tuck things away, like some of my desperate prayers not meant for display. I found a pink box at the craft store and bought some pink jewels to decorate the inside. When I opened it, the mirror surrounded by pink bling and butterflies reminded me that I'm a princess. I picked up a few other trinkets to add to the box and bring to my next counseling session. With excitement, I pulled out each item and shared with Deanna what it represented.

Then we moved on to the hard stuff. I shared all my confusion as a kid. During the fourth grade, I woke up to blood in my underwear. In fear, I went into my parents' room and tossed my underwear on the floor. My mom opened a medical book and showed me a picture of ovaries, which I thought were breasts. She asked if I had any questions. I shook my head no. She handed me a sanitary pad. "Congratulations, you are now a woman."

In my family, that would not be a reason to celebrate or say congratulations. Women were objects on display, expected to cook and clean. You could work, but you had many duties at home. I can still hear my grandpa yelling for my grandma and my dad yelling for my mom. They yelled their names over and over. My mom could be cleaning the bathroom with her hands covered in Comet but would stop to see what my dad needed.

"Make me some popcorn," he would say as he sat in his recliner watching television. Without a word, she would go into the kitchen to wash her hands and get his bowl of popcorn ready. Her facial expressions spoke volumes, and sometimes she would whisper, "One of these days."

When I went into the bathroom and opened the pad, instead of sticking it to my underwear, I stuck it to myself and later understood my painful and messy mistake. We didn't have tampons, so I never used them. At pool time, I avoided the water and got lost in a book instead. I never wanted to wear a swimsuit anyway.

I heard my older cousins talking about a girl missing her period and possibly being pregnant. This made me worry I might be pregnant the next month when my period didn't arrive as expected. I hadn't had sex and didn't understand how to make a baby, but being pregnant terrified me. Thankfully, my cycle started a few days later. I asked my dad to order "My First Period Kit," which came with sample pads and information about starting your period. He ordered it for me, and I learned more about my monthly cycle.

This fear of getting pregnant surfaced in various ways. After school, my sitter had a glass of refreshing grape Kool Aid for us to drink. I stopped drinking it, convinced if I drank it, I would get pregnant. My mom would pick me up and hear me say, "I'm so thirsty," but I couldn't tell her why.

Even though I didn't understand my menstrual cycle or how babies were made, I had full access to porn from the magazines openly displayed under my parents' bed. When I heard the song, "Centerfold" by the J. Giles band, I knew what it meant for an angel to be the centerfold. Those naked angels were on the pages that folded out to make posters in dirty magazines. Their perfect bodies were usually on the cover too.

I stared at my body and pinched the fat on my stomach, knowing I would never be like the angel in the centerfold. Their curves were perfect, and they hardly had any hair. Exposed in my shiny, blue unitard with no bra or underwear, I hated my body, especially in dance class when mirrors surrounded us. I could see the dirty parts of me with every twist and turn. At recital time, there were no mirrors. An audience would sit and watch my body jiggle on display. I had no idea what they were thinking or what they could see. But I knew my dad sat in the balcony watching me. Staring into his video camera. Recording it all. Zooming in on me.

As I shared all this, Deanna helped me get grounded and back in the present. "Let's talk about God in all of this."

I wrestled with doubt, confusion, and all the spiritual implications. If God promises retribution, what does it look like? How can He bring restoration? I had big questions that could only be answered when I brought Him into the story. I had always kept the abuse compartmentalized in a box far from God. I went to church and prayed, but the abuse and God did not go together. I tried to merge the two and find God in the abuse, wondering what He thought about it. In that search, one of the first things He showed me is that I'm a gift. Deanna helped me process this truth considering the abuse I experienced.

"Michelle, children are a gift from the Lord. What the person who opens the gift does with it doesn't diminish the giver."

At the beginning of my therapy, Deanna told me I could leave everything in an imaginary box so I could enjoy my family, then bring it with me each week for us to unpack. As I went deeper into counseling, this proved to be more difficult.

For the most part, Anthony stayed incredibly supportive and encouraging even in the worst moments. But we all have our limits. At one point, I became so self-focused I lived and breathed the abuse. It affected everything. I didn't want the kids to go outside because they might get hurt. I needed control. I'm sure it frustrated my husband.

I talked more openly and in detail with him about the abuse, but also about my own past and the many bad decisions I made in my youth. One night on our way to dinner, I casually mentioned that I cheated on him when we first started dating. I could tell by his expression he had no idea, even though I remembered where we were when I told him about hooking up.

"I thought you meant you kissed him," Anthony said.

I stared at him. I tried to remember exactly what I had said. Evidently, I didn't tell him the whole truth because he assured me he would've remembered. I didn't consider it lying. I considered it survival. But it had all been lies. Moments like this were where the lies and half-truths from my past piled high and threatened to destroy us. Our conversation escalated about how everything revolved around me.

Somewhere in our back-and-forth, Anthony said, "Well, if I had known then what I know now, I never would've dated you."

To say that comment crushed me wouldn't even touch the pain pounding through my body. He quickly said he didn't mean it. Too late. The voices in my head were already shouting. *This is why. It's going to get worse. You won't have anyone in your life when this is over. You are ruining everything!* I did my best to ignore the noise in my head and stay in the conversation with Anthony. I knew he sincerely wanted to be helpful and did not mean to hurt me, but those words screamed in my head until my next session.

When we were getting ready for bed that night, I took off my hot-pink watch and put it in my drawer. I put my princess sign in my Journey Box. I didn't want it all on display anymore. I didn't want it to be all about me in any way. Me, a fraud. I'd lied about myself my entire life. I didn't know the real me. What if no one liked her? Especially Anthony.

In the pitch dark, I pulled the covers over my head. The sad reality? I never had a choice. If I had a choice, I wouldn't be me either. If I could turn back time and make different decisions, I would. Even more, I wondered what my life would have looked like had the abuse never happened and where I would be today if I could truly say, "No, thankfully that never happened to me."

I brought this up at my next session with Deanna. I bit my lip and popped my fingers as I tried to form the sentences. "Maybe I wouldn't be so messed up if I'd never been abused. The mind games, control, and manipulation have hardwired my brain into thinking everyone has an agenda. I always need to be on full alert." I asked if she thought my brain could be fixed and if so, what about my full-alert paranoia and triggers?

She let me continue down the hopeless trail for a bit, then reminded me, "Michelle, look how far you have come. Yes, Anthony said something very hurtful, but he sincerely apologized. We all make mistakes. He's been super support- ive. This is hard on you, but he's exhausted trying to figure it all out. You've taken big steps, and we can rewire those thought patterns. What do you think it would look like if you had never been abused?"

"I have no idea. I've always thought I had a big *A* on my forehead that gave men a sign to do whatever they wanted to me. You know, like the *A* in the *Scarlet Letter.* Or maybe it's me. Maybe there's something in me that screams it. I don't know."

She probed deeper. "Tell me why you think that is the case."

I bit even harder into my lip and sat on both my hands to keep them still. I started to tell her, but then stopped.

She continued to look at me with her patient and gentle eyes, waiting for me to continue.

I shook my head. "This is bad. I really regret it. I had recently finished college. As an adult, the whole thing was so gross."

She continued to listen and did not move her papers or her eyes.

"I hate a lot of things about my body, but I really hate to shave. When I do, it grows right back. I wanted to get waxed, so I went to a nice salon for a consultation. The male esthetician asked me what I needed. I explained I didn't want to shave for a while. He said he could do dif- ferent designs like a landing strip. I said, 'No, I just want to wear a bathing suit.' He recommended I look at some magazines and said if I wanted to look like any of the naked women in them, he would do a design. He went on to make this seem normal and convinced me a lot of women do it. They start with a wax, then it gets fancy. He made it seem typical, like no big deal. He said we would do some sample waxing of certain areas to try it out. It would not be painful. He said he would be right back and for me to get completely undressed and lie on the table. When he entered the room again, he instructed me to relax. Then he took his fat, chunky fingers and trailed them along any areas that had hair. He started at my armpits and moved all the way down my body."

My breath caught, but Deanna nodded for me to go on.

"I completely froze and stared at the ceiling tiles, count-ing the dots on each tile. I could hear bits and pieces about how he has helped many women as he moved my legs apart and moved his hand. I wanted to sink through the floor and die. My body failed me. I hated myself and felt disgusting. As he left, he looked back and said, 'Be sure to bring any photos with you next time if you want to try something different.' I scrambled to find my underwear. There would be no next time. I cried all the way to my car."

At some point Deanna had handed me a tissue. I shred-ded it to pieces in my lap. I looked up and could see the fury in her eyes. "Michelle, listen to me. *Not* your fault."

I continued to wrap the pieces of tissue around my fingers and rip them even more as I whispered in disgust, "I just laid there. I didn't do anything. I didn't say anything."

She leaned in and spoke each word slowly. "Because that is what you were trained to do. You froze because of your fight, flight, or freeze response. Not because you did something wrong." She continued to explain the science behind it, but I grabbed the one phrase and let it play loudly in my mind. *Michelle, listen to me. Not your fault.*

Not my fault? I desperately wanted to believe those words.

On the way home, I stopped to pick up lunch and drove by the salon. I parked, sat in my car, and cried. At lunch, I told Anthony what I shared with Deanna.

He hugged me and said he loved me. Then he squeezed my hand and affirmed Deanna's words to me: *Not your fault.*

Maybe those words were really true.

The next week, I started group therapy with Deanna, another counselor, and several ladies. We used the book by Brené Brown called *I Thought It Was Just Me (But It Isn't)*. At one of the sessions, Deanna gave each of us a small craft box, some magazines, scissors, and glue. The assignment included cutting out words and images to glue on the inside and outside of the box.

The outside of the box displayed what we were comfortable with others knowing about us. These words represented how others see us and what we were willing to show them. Mostly public information.

The inside of the box contained private information. How we saw ourselves and what we did not want others to see or know about us. The images and words inside the box made us uncomfortable, especially if others knew about them.

The room suddenly filled with noise from the magazine pages flipping, scissors cutting, and pages ripping, all while music played softly in the background.

For me, words popped off the pages. Some were seemingly harmless, but very significant to me. We took the boxes home to finish them, and I continued to cut and paste away. The inside of my box contained shameful secrets, all so dark and dirty. Those words and images kept me chained to the darkness. I desperately longed to be free. When I opened the lid and looked at the bottom, three stick figures held hands with a child in the middle. Words surrounding the image said, *Oh, no, he didn't. Oh, yes, he did.*

Creating this box empowered me. I continued to bring it to my sessions. It helped me find words to share about how the abuse had affected my body, mind, and soul.

The biggest word I cut out for the box hid underneath the lid. *Secrets.* A word that summed up all the other words. The box opened now, with His light shining into the darkness.

The secrets were slowly coming out, one by one.

I made a C in conduct in the third grade. My parents scheduled a conference with my teacher. She told my parents I could beat up any boy in the class. She also suggested I acted like a mean tomboy and should wear dresses. After that conference, I learned that acting out in a bad way brought way too much attention. My life went a lot smoother and easier if teachers loved me. My final conduct grade improved significantly in her class and by the time I graduated from high school, I won the superlative trophy for "Teacher's Pet."

Chapter 12

TALITHA KOUM

Excited to show Deanna my finished box at my next appointment, I handed it to her before I even sat down and watched in anticipation as she opened it and looked inside. I wondered if she could see the memory behind every word.

She nodded, then said we could pick a few words and go from there.

I anxiously shared my other big news. Anthony's sister planned to visit in a few days. I planned to tell her my story. We had recently updated our will, and she needed to know so if something happened to us, she would be aware and help protect our kids. I rehearsed what I would say to her, but had no idea how she would respond. I worried she would think badly of me. Besides Anthony, she would be the first family member I shared with. This seemed like a big deal.

Anthony encouraged me to tell his sister and said he would be there to help me. I let him see inside my box. We talked about some of the words. He knew how hard I worked to get better and encouraged me to keep going. He would say, "It's going to get better. We will get through this together." I thought this might destroy our marriage, but in reality, it brought us closer. Sure, there were struggles along the way, but at least I no longer had to hide secrets and pretend.

The good news I shared in my next session included my plans to see Beth Moore in Greensboro that weekend with a group of ladies from church. We all loved doing her Bible studies together, so this would be a special treat. I couldn't wait to hear her message. I thought if the opportunity presented itself, I might share my box with some of the ladies. Deanna encouraged me to trust God's timing.

This turned out to be one of the lighter sessions where I held my head high and shoulders back. I sat up straight the entire time and made eye contact. It made me realize I had actually made progress. Usually, I left feeling stuck in a memory from long ago, but not this time. I moved forward, taking baby steps toward freedom.

We said our goodbyes and I left, smiling all the way to my car. But before I could even make it out of the parking lot, I struggled again. My pounding heart ached while anxiety and panic permeated my entire being. The mean voices in my head argued loudly over how I would ruin everything by spilling these secrets.

When I turned on the radio to drown them out, they introduced a song from *Sister Act 2: Back in the Habit* called "His Eye Is on the Sparrow" by Lauren Hill and Tanya Blount. I had heard the song before, but not like this. I turned it up even louder and hummed along at first, mumbling a few words. As I continued down the interstate in the sunlight, I sang at the top of my lungs about being happy and free.

I sang along, deep in worship.

That's when I heard a gentle whisper, *free at forty.*

Free at forty? I had no idea what *free at forty* meant. And since we were only days away from my birthday, it seemed impossible.

Then I heard it again, *free at forty*. What would it even look like? How could I possibly be free by then?

Free at forty. Impossible. But I sure liked the sound of it.

As I packed for the Beth Moore conference, I decided not to take my box because I didn't want it to get messed up. I opened it and snapped pictures of the inside so I could show the pictures if I decided to share with anyone.

On the way to Greensboro, I talked about making the box and how much it helped me. I even showed the ladies the picture of the lid where I had put the biggest word *Secrets*, explaining the rest of the box contained many secrets.

We made our way into the arena and waited for the conference to start. We were in the upper-level section, and as the intro video came on, the large screen in front of us displayed the word *Secrets*. The message for the weekend involved the impact of secrets in our lives. Timely for many, but right on time for me.

At the end of the Saturday session, we had a big celebration. There were beach balls bouncing around throughout the arena. Beautiful pieces of confetti spilled from the ceiling. I gathered a few pieces to put in my journey box because I wanted to remember everything.

I couldn't wait to get home and see my kids. I missed them so much, and I always felt guilty when away. We had a delightful dinner together, then stayed up a little late even though we had to get up early for church.

The next morning I dropped our youngest off at the nursery and made it to the sanctuary before the pastor started his sermon. While I flipped through my Bible to find the Scripture reference, he said, "Today I want to talk to you about the secret healings of Jesus ... and how some were public and some were private." I stopped thumbing the pages and looked up. He started in Mark 5 with the story of the woman with the bleeding issue. Then he moved on to the little girl in Mark 5. They thought she had died. But Jesus showed up. "He took her by the hand and said to her, 'Talitha Koum,' which means 'Little girl, I say to you, get up!'" (NIV).

Those words illuminated on the page of my Bible. My heart started racing.

He continued reading as I followed along. "Immediately, the girl stood up and began to walk around. She was twelve years old" (Mark 5:42 NIV).

I thought of the little girl inside me. We were connecting. I loved her. I had a picture of her on my phone and computer to remind me to fight for her on days when I wanted to give up. I opened my phone, looked at her picture, and cried, imagining Jesus whispering to the heart of the little girl inside of me, "Talitha Koum! Little girl, I say to you, get up!"

She and I were ready.

There would be no more hiding or cowering in a dark closet filled with lies and shame. I imagined her beside me holding my hand. Now we were one, and together we were fierce.

After church, my daughter and I made a picture with a pink crown on it and the words, *Talitha Koum*. We used all the confetti from the Beth Moore conference to make a colorful border to frame the edges. I wanted to share this with her when she got older and explain how those two words convinced me Jesus heals little girls, including LG.

A few days later, Anthony's sister came to visit. I had dropped my car off for an oil change. She drove me there to pick it up. At a stop sign, I looked in my rearview mirror and saw her behind me, smiling. Once I told her, I could not take it back. What would she think of me? I debated not telling her at all, but as I looked ahead again, I saw a beautiful bird on a sign in front of me. I snapped a picture and remembered "His Eye Is on the Sparrow." I knew Jesus watched over me. I smiled in the mirror at my sister-in-law as we headed home.

We went straight into the living room and sat down. Anthony and I were on one couch and his sister on the other. He explained our will. I looked at him intently, hoping he would keep talking so I wouldn't have to say anything. Then he said, "Michelle has something she would like to share with you."

I bit my bottom lip and turned to face Jenna. She tilted her head and leaned toward me, looking me in the eye. When I started talking, the words tumbled out. "Jenna, my dad sexually abused me throughout my childhood."

Her eyes widened in shock, but she continued to listen. When I stopped talking, I braced myself for her response.

Her first words were, "I'm so proud of you." She explained she knew how tough it had been for me to share with her because she had recently completed the Darkness to Light training with her Volleyball Club. She said she believed me and knew I did nothing wrong. She even expressed her thankfulness to have me in her life as her brother's wife. She also considered me to be a wonderful wife and mother.

I had witnessed others disclosing their abuse to family, which did not go well. But Jenna said everything right. At the time, I had not heard of Darkness to Light training, but I could tell she knew a lot. I believed I needed to tell her first because of the will we had set up, but now I think sharing with her first gave me the confidence to share with other family members. It also helped me see that God would lead me and show me the next steps. He prepared me with the song "His Eye Is on the Sparrow" and the bird on the sign.

He gave me the courage to tell her. I knew His presence surrounded me.

God prepared Jenna with the Darkness to Light training. She knew all about the devastating effects of childhood sexual abuse. She knew what to say and how to respond. She called me brave. She shared some of what she had learned in her training and how others had experienced abuse as well. She knew many suffered in silence. This recent training remained fresh in her mind.

God's perfect timing. Again.

Before she left, she hugged me and said, "You are so strong. I'm so proud of you."

I beamed as my head hit the pillow, and I actually slept. Relief filled me because it went well, but also because Jenna knew to protect my kids if something happened to us.

I wore a bright pink shirt and a big smile to my counseling session later in the week. Deanna tilted her head and grinned as she came around the corner to greet me in the waiting room. I jumped to my feet and headed toward her. I started talking before she closed the door.

"I did it! I told Anthony's sister. And guess what? She had completed the Darkness to Light training and understood. It went so well. Anthony stayed very engaged and supportive. There's only one thing ... I feel bad in some ways. Like maybe I mistreated my dad by sharing with others first. I betrayed him."

Deanna quickly directed my thoughts to the need to celebrate that sharing with Jenna went well. "Sometimes sharing can be traumatic, but this went well. You do not have to feel like you betrayed your dad. This is your pattern of protecting him. His actions have consequences. It is not your responsibility to carry this for him. Let's focus on the biblical reality, speaking the truth in love and walking in the light. That is what you did."

I stared at her and tried to focus on the truth, but the spiritual concepts were all tangled in my mind. *What about being submissive? What about obedience and honor? He told me never to tell. What about children obey your parents? What about those truths?*

But instead I said, "Anthony thinks I need to confront my dad and tell my family. He will do it with me and help me, but I don't even know what to say to my dad."

"We can work on it. You can decide who you will share with and what you will share with each person. But for your dad, you can tell him directly what secrets you are no longer keeping."

"Well," I replied, "that may take a while."

The tickling torture game. What started as a bout of laughter turned into being unable to catch my breath. Frozen. We were out in the open, usually on the living room floor. I tried to yell, but sound escaping changed nothing. At some point, my mom would yell, "Stop aggravating her!" Not much longer. Eventually, he stopped. Relief.

Chapter 13

FREE AT FORTY

I arrived at the local pizza shop to have lunch with my Sunday school teacher. I shared some of my story with her then told her my plans.

"I intend to meet with my mom and tell her first. Then I will tell my brother. After that I will meet with my dad."

She let me elaborate on the specifics over my plate of cold pizza. When I asked what she thought, she simply said, "Pray about it. Trust the Lord's timing. You have a plan, but it may be better for you to meet with your dad first to avoid him hearing it from someone else instead of you."

She prayed with me. As she prayed, I knew my plans were changing. I agreed with her about confronting him first. She gave me a big hug and told me the Lord would go before me.

I couldn't wait to tell Deanna I had shared my story again with someone. It went well this time too. She celebrated my progress and reminded me everyone may not respond the same.

All my excitement vanished when I brought up a memory that happened a few weeks before the first time I confronted my dad on biscuit day.

I had come home for the weekend from college and went out to a local bar with a friend. The bar used to be a church, but had since been filled with high-top tables and loud country music. We sang and danced. I didn't want to go home, so we stayed until they turned the lights on bright and announced the closing of the bar.

My mom and dad had briefly separated at the time. She lived on her own in an apartment. I stumbled into the house at 2:30 in the morning, trying my best to be quiet because I did not want to wake up my dad. As I tiptoed through the dark kitchen, I ran directly into him, standing in the dark in only his underwear.

My heart sank when he said, "I've been waiting for you."

I looked at Deanna then back at the window as I saw it all play out. Saying I had a headache didn't stop him. It seemed as if I were watching it on a TV screen in slow motion. No fast-forward button to push. My lips trembled as I described every detail.

"A few weeks later, my mom came back home. Dad told her he would give her one more chance. She could come back home, but if she ever left again, that would be it. There would be no more chances. I hoped she stayed because I never wanted to be alone with him like that again. Biscuit day happened before she left again, this time for good."

I quit talking and sat there with tears pouring down my face, on sensory overload as all that had been bottled up for years in silence finally made its way out, word by awful word. At times, the images were so horrific that I longed to believe it never happened. The thought hit me again, *maybe I've lost my mind and made it all up.* In the beginning—with a flashback or two—I battled with this constantly. In fact, this made it easier to push it all the way down and pretend—and always with a smile.

The truth is, in public, he acted like a fantastic dad. Always there. He attended all my dance recitals and sporting events.

He provided for our family. He encouraged me. He's the one who told me I could do anything. He took us to church and stayed involved in our lives. Charming. Successful. Great sense of humor. Everyone loved him. I loved him.

I held tightly to the good times with him when others were around because focusing on the best times helped me survive. But now, as a thirty-nine-year-old woman, I relived the horror of all he would say and do to me when we were alone and behind closed doors. In these memories, his eyes suddenly turned dark as if someone flipped a light switch, filling me with absolute terror.

The flashbacks were like taking a box of puzzle pieces, shaking it up, and then letting the pieces fly out onto the ground all at once. Easy to ignore when I looked at one awful piece because I could pick up three good pieces and dismiss the bad. But when the awful pieces covered the entire floor and started connecting, the full image of the abuse began to form and could not be denied.

Even in my own mind, I had no proof. No DNA. No witnesses. Plus, I didn't want to believe it, so it became easier for me to doubt. If I doubted myself, I wondered if anyone would believe me. But it really didn't matter. I believed me now, and with each flashback, I believed myself even more.

At Zumba® one day, we were dancing away to the song "Good Feeling" by Flo Rida. Because it was one of our regular dance songs, I had it memorized, so I didn't have to think about the next move or focus on the teacher. Letting go in the movement and singing along, I suddenly stopped. I recalled something strange my dad asked me. A simple question. I had no idea how it fit, but I knew it all connected. I couldn't wait to share it with Deanna. I finished the class almost robotically. When I came home, I Googled the sentence.

Nothing. But yet it seemed important. I couldn't think of any other reason he would ask me did I "catch a feeling" other than the obvious.

I looked forward to the ladies' Bible study at church each week. I didn't always say much, but it comforted me to be with others because I hungered for truth and light after swimming so long in lies and darkness. A few of them knew my story, and they were praying for me. After we finished Beth Moore's *Breaking Free* study together, we were working through her Daniel study.

The lights dimmed in the room for the video to begin. I took a big sip from my Diet Coke bottle. I stared at the screen as Beth emphatically shared about how "we are holy vessels, but sometimes our holy vessels are used to toast an unholy cause."

She had my attention. My hands shook. My eye started twitching. I didn't feel holy, and I certainly didn't consider myself a holy vessel. But I could definitely relate to being used for an unholy cause.

Beth stared straight at us as she talked. At the end, she had us stand to our feet and repeat after her as she read a declaration of holiness over our lives. My knees threatened to give out. My lips hardly moved to declare, "I am a holy vessel."

My body threatened to explode, and I wanted to sink through the floor.

As soon as she said the last word, I grabbed my books and ran to my car. I collapsed over the steering wheel in tears. All the way home, I desperately prayed out loud, "God, help me believe You. I believe you in my head. Please help me believe You in my heart. I don't feel holy, and I want to believe it. Please help me, God. Please help me to believe. Help my unbelief."

I spoke these words out loud as I prayed. It reminded me of the father in Mark 9:24, who asked Jesus to heal his son and said, "I do believe; help me overcome my unbelief!" (NIV).

When I shared this with Deanna at our next session, I handed her the declaration to read because I had looked it up and written it down using my name. I still had a hard time saying it, much less believing it. She encouraged me to focus on and memorize truth when I struggled with lies about myself. Sincerely grappling with this truth, I asked, "How can I be holy when I'm so dirty? I did so many bad things. I made bad choices. All my bad behavior supports his abuse. Maybe I brought it on."

Deanna sighed. "Michelle, God is helping you strip away all this self-hatred. He wants you to be in tune with your worth and who He created you to be. Your bad behavior does not support your dad's abuse. The abuse made you feel dirty, but you are not dirty. You are holy. Can you see the difference?"

"Maybe." I could see my daughter as holy. Maybe the little girl inside of me could be holy too.

Back in my car, I sat there for a minute to gather myself. As I went to type a note, a text came through from Anthony saying, *See you soon*, with a picture of my kids smiling and holding their arms out under a beautiful rainbow.

With my birthday only days away—and me more anxious than usual—I made plans with a friend to get together after Zumba®. Months before, she had hugged me and whispered, "I see how hard you work."

I went to her house. We sat together on the couch to catch up. At first, we made small talk about the kids. Then I told her about the challenges I faced. As I shared my story with her, I never teared up. For the very first time, I didn't cry.

She hugged me and said she believed me, and she believed *in* me. She loved being my friend. Even with my taboo and awful situation, she stood with me. My entire being felt safe and loved. As I pulled out of her driveway, it dawned on me that I never told her to keep it a secret. The voice in my head immediately started in on me, *You've done it now.* But this time I quickly fired back, "Shut up!"

I woke up at four a.m. and started typing into my phone what I would say to my dad if I ever confronted him. Roughly twenty sentences long. After typing, I fell back asleep. I had therapy that morning, so I planned to share my words with Deanna. The thought of confronting him made my eyes twitch and my insides shake. It seemed impossible. Suddenly, my accusing thoughts came back. *What if I'm wrong? What if I made this all up?*

Since I had never told anyone, I didn't have any evidence except the thoughts and images in my head and what my body shouted at me. I tried to think of someone I would have possibly said anything to about the abuse.

Only one possibility came to mind. One of my best friends from college had seen me at my worst in drunken stupors—the one I called when I blacked out somewhere and needed a ride home. She knew I had peed on our carpet when too drunk to make it to the bathroom. She had witnessed the worst of me as I tried to numb my pain. As much as I drank around her, I figured I might have slipped and mentioned something at some point.

I nervously dialed her number, relieved when I got her voicemail. But before I could finish leaving her a message, she called me back.

"Hey, Res. How's it going?" I asked as cheerfully as I could.

"Good, Mik. What's up with you?" she asked.

"Listen, I don't have a lot of time right now, but I need your help. Back when we were in college, did I ever share anything awful with you?"

"What?"

"I know I got drunk a lot, and you saw me at my worst. I blacked out many nights and couldn't remember anything, so I wondered if I ever talked about something shameful. Like a secret."

"Are you talking about your dad?"

My heart dropped to my toes. I almost threw the phone as if it were on fire. I cleared my throat to be able to speak. "I told you? Really?"

"Yes, Mik. You told me. Don't you remember? You came home from counseling upset because your counselor planned to move to another state. She told you how telling someone your story might make you feel better. So, we went to the tennis courts and sat on the metal bench by the graveyard. You told me."

I cried as she described memories in detail that I had been wrestling with for months. I could almost feel the hard bench and the warm sun shining on us as tennis balls bounced in the background. Her face displayed shock, making me feel even more green. Telling someone did not make me feel better.

"What happened after that?" I asked.

"You never brought it up again. I didn't know what to say and figured everything turned out okay. Your dad still came around. You acted like nothing happened so I thought you were fine. But I can tell you this. I've talked with coworkers and friends about protecting their kids. I shared how I knew someone who had been abused and no one would have ever suspected it. You have no idea how your story impacted many young girls, including my own."

I could hardly breathe, much less talk.

"Mik, I'm sorry. I didn't want to bring it up again unless you did. And you never did."

"Please don't apologize. You didn't do anything wrong. You have no idea how much this has helped me. I love you, and I'm sorry I dumped it all on you back then. I'm thankful if it helped in any way. It has certainly helped me today. I'll share more later, but again, thank you so much."

My feet seemed way ahead of my body as I made my way to Deanna's door. "I told someone," I blurted out. "I'm already free. He's the one who will be shaking."

She raised her eyebrows, evidently waiting for me to say more.

In my usual fashion I blurted again, "So much has happened." I sat on the edge of the couch with my chin up and said, "I feel empowered." I told her about sharing with my friend and about the conversation with my roommate at UNC. Before she could even respond, I said, "And this morning I woke up at four a.m. and typed exactly what I will say to my dad if I confront him. I woke up, grabbed my phone, typed it, and fell back asleep. When I woke up again, it seemed like a dream. But sure enough, I found it in the notes on my phone. God gave me the words. Do you want me to read it to you?"

She shook her head. "Wow, you have had an eventful week."

I read my notes to her and said I believed free at forty would really happen. My dad had been reaching out to me, but I ignored his efforts.

Deanna liked that I had what I planned to say written out on my phone. She said if I needed to read it out word for word, that would work.

The thought of it filled me with angst and anticipation. I would only be thirty-nine for a few more hours.

I woke up to my kids singing "Happy Birthday" to me. It turned out to be a happy day. I still ignored Dad's voicemails. After work, I met a friend to do Zumba® with students at a local middle school. In one of the moves, I turned around and imagined several of the young girls with tape over their mouths. It made me tear up. I knew in a roomful of so many girls, some of them would share my story. They were smiling behind their horror, like I did. It angered me but also filled me with a passion for helping them.

Afterward, we decided to stop for chips and salsa. When I walked into the restaurant, I saw balloons, a cake, and familiar faces. Surprised, I quickly scanned the faces to make sure I didn't see my dad.

We had a wonderful night of laughter and fun. Anthony and the kids were there. They gathered close when I closed my eyes to blow out the candle. I made my wish.

We arrived home with full hearts and tummies. I had a wonderful birthday. I fell asleep *forty*, but I still didn't feel free.

On my way to Zumba® early the next morning, a friend sat at the stoplight across from me. She texted, *I'm home by myself this weekend if you need me to babysit.*

Such a random text. She had posted on Facebook that her husband had taken the girls so she could enjoy her Mother's Day weekend. I texted back, *I saw your post on Facebook. I wouldn't ask you to babysit when you are getting a break. Ha!*

After Zumba®, I rushed home for my daughter's soccer game. We were waiting for my oldest son to get home from a friend's house. He came in a few minutes late with a gift for me. He had apparently asked his friend's mom to stop by the Hallmark store to get me a gift, even asking her to pay for it. He walked in full of excitement when he gave it to me. Such a thoughtful and sweet gesture.

I opened the bag and found a purple flower in a purple vase that said, *Special Day ... Special You.* He excitedly showed me where to push the button to get the flower to open. He pushed it, and the blooms fell open to reveal the message *Happy You Day.* I gave him a big hug, then we all loaded up to head to the game.

When we returned home, my husband checked the mail, then handed it to me as he turned into the driveway. I immediately recognized my dad's familiar handwriting and noticed the envelope had no stamp. We had missed him.

I texted him to thank him for the card and asked if he planned to head home.

He replied, *No, I'm coming back by and will see you in about forty-five minutes.*

I had less than an hour to get ready. I did not want my kids to be there. I called my friend from the stoplight and asked if we could please drop them off for a bit.

"Sure," she said.

We delivered the kids, walked back into the house, and I started pacing the living room floor. Too quiet. I turned on some music. I played a song that had steadied me for months called "Keep Me" by Patrick Dopson. I sang along in a loud voice. It became my heart's cry for Jesus to help me. I clapped and prayed as if I were about to enter a sports arena and wanted to get pumped up. When I dropped to my knees in worship, God filled me with enormous peace.

I stood up and looked in the mirror as the rocks crunched in the driveway. My dad would walk in any minute. Free at forty would happen shortly.

Anthony met him at his car and asked him to come inside. I stood waiting as they walked toward me. I thought my chest would split open when I looked into the eyes of my Goliath.

Anthony stood beside me. "Michelle has something she needs to say to you."

Dad looked at me, brows raised.

Terrified, I could barely open my mouth. I finally whispered, "You sexually abused me, and I'm not keeping the secret anymore." Then I remembered Deanna telling me to read from my phone. I whipped it out and spoke louder.

"I look at my kids, and I see them as a gift. I feel bad when I raise my voice at them, yet you used me like a piece of trash. And that is how you made me feel—like a piece of trash. It did not make me feel special, loved, worthy, or cherished. Instead of caring for me, you lied, manipulated, touched me, watched me, and ultimately raped me."

I took in a quick breath and kept going.

"Those three women in Cleveland who were found trapped in a stranger's home for ten years—horrible! Tragic! Unbelievable! This stranger kidnapped them and left them chained in a house. Their parents looked for them. For me, you were not a stranger. You were my parent. All I had. And I had to learn to go outside of the house and pretend to be normal. I had nowhere to run. I had to hope people would not look at me and know. I had to work extra hard to appear happy. You treated me like a piece of trash. You damaged me. But the good news is I'm healing. I'm in counseling now and group therapy. I have spent a lot of time and money understanding I'm worthy. I'm a gift, not a piece of trash. I'm a wife. I'm a mother. And I'm a precious, treasured, and loved daughter of Jesus Christ, my Father. So please do not call, visit, or interact online with us—especially with my children. You can write us through the mail only. And don't *ever* call me doll baby again. Ever."

I finally lifted my head and looked at my dad, his expression unreadable as his eyes darkened.

After an awkward pause, he said, "I'm sorry." He looked over at Anthony and acknowledged he had made mistakes in his life. Then he turned back to me and apologized, again.

After another long pause, Anthony said, "Please. What she said, I'm asking you to honor that right now."

"I understand."

Anthony moved closer to me and put his arm around my shoulders. "We have to go pick up our kids now. Michelle needed to say this. She will be fine. She has a family who loves her. I love her."

My dad stood rigid with his arms crossed over his belly. He shifted his gaze to Anthony and said, "I know you do."

Then he glanced at me, "Honestly, I love you too. I really do. I always have. There is nothing short about that." Our eyes had their own conversation. I could feel the chill of his stare when he looked my way. I wondered if he felt mine.

He looked back at Anthony, "There were some things that happened that never should've happened, and I ... ya know ... take whatever responsibility I need to take."

"She needs time."

"I understand." As Dad turned to leave he said, "Anything I can do, let me know."

He seemed much smaller to me as he walked out. Elated, I no longer shook. My heartbeat slowed down. Anthony wisely let me take in the moment. We both knew deep down that Dad did not give me the sincere, emotional apology I needed. It reminded me of a deer-caught-in-the-headlights moment. There were no tears, and his eyes spoke volumes to me. But at least he didn't deny it and call me a liar.

Finally free—free at forty! The lies and secrets that had suffocated me were all out in the open now.

My husband and I left the house and were on our way to pick up the kids when he said, "Michelle, get your phone. Quick. Take a picture." He pointed to the car in front of us.

I smiled and snapped away. The license plate said THNK PNK.

Wow, only God. He knew I needed to remember. Hard things are always hard. So always THNK PNK.

We picked up the kids and went to a party with friends. I walked on cloud nine, laughing and having a great time from the adrenaline rush. I slept peacefully and woke up with a smile on my face ... at least for a little while.

I sang the new song "Against All Odds" by Phil Collins in my mind as I mowed the lot beside our house. I had heard a girl a few years older than me commit-ted suicide. They said she did it because she missed her recently deceased dad. The sad thoughts in my mind made straight lines and sudden turns much like the lawnmower plowing through the field. The hum of the mower and the smell of grass tugged me back into reality. I believed he knew me better than anyone else, and I couldn't imagine my life without him.

Chapter 14

COLORED PENCILS AND LYRICS

At some point, the guilt crept back in. I betrayed my dad, and he probably hated me now. But instead of trying to numb the pain and heartache, I sat with it for a while. The voices were back in my head, meaner than ever. *What are you going to tell your kids? What's your plan now? You have ruined everything, and why? I hope you're happy.* I didn't have it in me to tell them to shut up this time.

Thankfully, I had scheduled a counseling session before my group therapy meeting. I arrived early, so I stopped at a HomeGoods store. Tears poured down my face as I walked down the aisles, touching the soft towels and smelling the candles. I thought about the pain from the weekend and felt incredibly wounded.

On the way back to my car, I spotted a small bird in the parking lot two spaces away. It did not move and barely opened its eyes. It almost looked dead. I stood there taking pictures of it. It let me get very close, and I wondered out loud, "God, what are you saying to me? Pink skies, birds ... you have my attention." The wounded part had me a little uneasy. "Are you telling me I'm wounded?"

I switched to video to show the quiet bird and how close it sat to my car. Then, as I filmed for the next forty-nine seconds, the bird started chirping, hopping around, and stretching its wings. It even awkwardly attempted to fly. I started the car to follow, but lost sight of it. I turned the engine off.

I laughed and cried. I called a friend and exclaimed, "I'm so wounded. But eventually, I will fly. I need to start chirping and stretching my wings. My steps may be awkward or look different at first, but eventually I will fly.

At our last group therapy session, we were all given a small sheet of paper to draw on and to share with the group. Usually, I stayed pretty quiet and reserved, but I think the Lord used the bird to give me an extra dose of courage for this session.

In the middle of my paper, I wrote the words *Childhood Sexual Abuse*. In a circle around those words in green, I wrote the lies and how they made me feel like *trash, bad girl, damaged goods, unloved*, and *not enough*. In a circle around those words, I wrote the truth in pink. *I am not alone. I am special, worthy, and God loves me*. Along the sides I wrote, *I am not afraid. I will talk. What you used to harm me, God will use for good. I have a voice!*

As one of the first to share, I held the paper up and read every word out loud to the group. Shame covered me but also hope and a strong desire to soar.

As I attempted to organize my bookshelf over the weekend, I came across a book for my oldest son called *Mom Remembers: A Treasury of Memories for My Child*. This journal contained memories for him. I didn't finish writing in it, of course, because I never do. So a lot of the pages were blank.

I flipped through it to the page regarding my parents. I had written, *They were strict about everything. I would get grounded quite a bit, and one time in college, I got spanked hard with a belt for talking back.*

In the paragraph where I had to write about my dad, I said *He encouraged me and gave me a lot of confidence. He taught me to never give up.* Ten years ago, I wrote that in the book, and it made me so sad to read it. Getting spanked hard with a belt while in college for talking back left a significant mark on me, enough to include it in this memory book. I mentioned talking back. I didn't mention biscuit day.

It's also interesting that I said he taught me to never give up. I'm not sure if he ever said it to me, but I knew the little girl inside me had modeled it for me by surviving. She remained strong.

I attended a special church service dedicated to sexual abuse. Clayton King preached a sermon on Tamar and then played a video of a woman who had been abused. In it she shared her story. When she came on stage, Clayton introduced her as his wife, Shari King.

In the video, she painted a self-portrait. It reminded me of the little girl photo I carried with me. I kept thinking about what it would've been like to experience a powerful message like this as a child. What would have happened if someone shared their story like that when I sat in church with my dad?

Shari's painting inspired me to draw my self-portrait from the little girl picture on my phone. At home, I pulled out my colored pencils and attempted to draw little Michelle. I tried about three times but could never make her look young enough. She always looked older than the picture.

This became a real struggle for me. I always felt older, and I drew myself that way. I couldn't draw or even imagine being a little girl. I knew more about *Hustler* and *Playboy* than I knew about Barbie dolls.

I shared the drawing with Deanna, realizing there were other survivors out there too. Not alone. I told her about reading *Hush* by Nicole Braddock Bromley and her story of sexual abuse. It pained me to know others were abused, but it also convinced me that so many suffered in a code of silence and shame.

I reached in my purse and unfolded a ripped napkin I had scribbled on to figure out my age when my dad first raped me. Twelve. Twelve years old (almost thirteen) when red-orange happened. It reminded me again of Talitha Koum. That twelve-year-old girl heard Jesus say to her, "Talitha Koum, little girl I say to you, get up." It was as if Jesus said Talitha Koum to the twelve-year-old hurting little girl inside of me. "It's not over yet. We have a ways to go. But I'm here. I'm here to help you get up."

Part of my struggle came because I believed myself to be somewhat responsible and didn't want to release myself from complying. At the time, I considered *rape* a strong word for me to use. I certainly didn't like it or enjoy it, but I also didn't stop it. I told Deanna, "It's not like he displayed violence. He didn't force or hurt me. But I didn't say no."

When I finished piling on the excuses to justify my thoughts, Deanna asked me to consider my options. What choices did I have? What does force look like?

In the end, I understood I had been a twelve-year-old girl who learned at an early age to be compliant. I never had the choice to go against him, even when the abuse became intense and painful. I survived by being compliant. Otherwise, the risk became too great.

My brother planned a splash party. I knew my dad would be there, and my kids would want to go. I also knew I needed to tell my brother and my mom about the abuse. Anthony said he would help me, but I didn't want to do anything yet and mess up the party. Deanna helped me set boundaries with my dad by reminding me I could always leave early or spend time in the bathroom if needed.

We went to the party. I never said a word to my dad. I didn't even look at him. Thankfully, no one seemed to notice. My mom mentioned she had never seen me smile so much. The day actually turned out to be fun. The kids were tired on the way home. From the back of the car, I could hear one of them singing, "Are You Sleeping?" I used to sing the song about "Brother John" in the car with my dad as a little girl. We were smiling and happy—a nice memory of him being a good dad to me—but the guilt was always there. A tear slipped down my face. Anthony noticed and reached for my hand. I said, "I wish I'd never said anything about the abuse. I'm going to destroy my entire family."

He had seen me flip-flop like this before, but he challenged me again to snap back into reality when he reminded me, "This is bigger than you, and you are not destroying your family. It's not your fault."

I sighed and turned up the radio. "Sad Eyes" by Robert John started playing. I could see my dad standing by his stack of albums and record player, singing and dancing in the living room. I abruptly turned the radio off and fell asleep with my head against the window.

I dreamed we were back at the splash party. I could not move or speak. I tried to talk but couldn't say a word. No one knew why I couldn't move or talk, but Anthony picked me up in his arms and carried me away from the party. When I woke up, the radio played quietly while the kids slept soundly in the back. I smiled at Anthony, thankful he stood by me even in my dreams.

A few days after the party, I talked to my mom. She asked me a question about my dad and mentioned where he worked. "Did you know he changed jobs?"

I tried to change the subject but finally admitted, "No, I haven't talked to him. I don't talk to him anymore."

"What do you mean you don't talk to him anymore?" she quickly retorted.

I tried to avoid the rest of her questions. I kept saying I had to go. It turned out to be a quick conversation. As we were about to say goodbye, she said, "I don't care what he's done. He's still your dad."

I let the full depth of those words sit in my throat for a minute. Too hard to swallow. The guilt, confusion, fear, and rage bubbled up like bile and made me want to vomit.

On my way to therapy, a new song called "Radioactive" came on the radio by Imagine Dragons. I turned it up loud as the lyrics pumped fresh courage deep inside my veins. I arrived a little early and had time to pull up the video on YouTube. I sat there speechless, watching a little pink bear take down the Goliaths.

I told Deanna all about the song and how it made me stronger. At most of my sessions, I came in with a song or two to discuss. Some of them triggered flashbacks while others empowered me to take the next step in my journey. I liked the beats, but the lyrics and the power of each word pumped emotions through my body and give me permission to *feel*, even for a moment.

When younger, I filled forty-nine-cents wide-ruled-spiral notebooks from Roses with song lyrics instead of writing in journals. We didn't have Google back then, so I had to press pause on the cassette tape player of my jam box and write down each word, then press rewind and do it all again. By the time I finished writing out the song, I had the lyrics memorized. The powerful words whispered pieces of my story to a stranger with no consequences. Anyone reading my pages would see lyrics to a song, but they were so much more to me. I could speak lyrics and sing songs and say words that helped me make sense of my world. Those notebooks whispered their secrets to me, and I sang my secrets back to them. We connected, music and me. The comforting gift of music gave me companionship in a lonely space.

I started a private board on Pinterest called Lyrical Moments and made the cover photo a picture of a jam box with the words, *Life is a Mixtape*. I told Deanna about it and how the pieces of those song lyrics were a peek into the secrets of my heart and soul. Those lyrics were the songs I had written in my notebooks and seared into my memory. For me, every song had a good or bad memory attached to it. I can hear a song now and remember the emotion or memory that went with it. Flipping through the radio stations became like jumping back and forth to different chapters in my life, with all the *feels*.

I bought a smash journal and used it to cut and paste song lyrics. Google made it easy. I printed the lyrics mostly, but it electrified me to grab a pen and write each word in a notebook to see my secrets unfold with my own hand.

I showed the book to Deanna and shared how each lyric related to my experiences. They were songs, but for me, they were my ultimate truth-tellers. For example, "Every Breath You Take" by the Police sang to my heartache of being constantly watched and stared at with no privacy. I sat with this song open for a minute and stared at the words.

My heart pounded as I described how being watched reminded me of a normalized jump scare. You know, the part in a movie that suddenly shocks you and makes you jump. It's like watching the same movie over and over—knowing what's coming but still jumping every time.

Everything stayed quiet for a minute as my own jump scares popped into my head. "Whether in the tub, the shower, getting dressed in my room, sleeping, or putting on makeup in front of the mirror, I knew to expect him to be quietly peeking, but it still startled me every time. Every move I made, he watched me."

"Let's go back to the lyrics," Deanna suggested.

"'Hungry Like the Wolf" by Duran Duran would play on the radio and taunt me like a bad dream. It made me feel hunted, stalked even, by a hungry wolf with dark eyes who camouflaged his voracious appetite. Songs would trigger me at times, but they also played a significant role in my healing. The lyrics and deeply ingrained images from music videos that played on MTV helped me express what my younger self couldn't say."

"Which is ..."

"Think about it. A child. A daughter. But also prey. Both protected and hunted—and not a game. I desperately wanted to forget it all, yet could not stop remembering. My sleep had always been tainted by recurring nightmares of being chased in the darkness. Always running. Always afraid. Exhausted."

Deanna nodded. "And the songs helped."

"I wanted to be safe and feel secure. God sheltered me in the storms and gave me new songs. These songs encouraged me to stop running and trying to hide from the darkness. I kept "Light 'em Up" by the Fallout Boys on repeat for a while. I would sing along with the volume turned up. God also gave me deliverance lyrics and the hope to know and believe that He sheltered me in the shadow of His wings, even in the darkness. I kept a playlist on my phone, and I named it Healing Moments. I heard 'Take Me to the King" by Tamela Mann and added it immediately. I told Anthony when I die, I want him to play this song at least twice at my funeral. Loud. These songs resonated deeply with my pain, but they also pointed me to His light and His hope. When I sang the words out loud, I knew He surrounded me. I believe He brought me this far, and

He has me in His hand. Slowly, I have understood how He has held me in His arms all along."

At the end of the session, I told Deanna about my mom's response to me not talking to my dad and how her remark made me think I should never tell her.

"Did you tell her anything?" Deanna asked.

"No. I kept avoiding her and trying to get off the phone. I dodged all her questions."

"Well, honestly, her response is not fully informed. You shouldn't take her statement to heart because at this point, you can't assume she knows."

My eyes grew wide. I physically shuddered, thinking of how hard it would be to tell her. Even harder to think about how she would respond. Would she believe me? I saw myself little again, standing in his bedroom, looking up at him as he warned me and helped me understand I could never tell anyone, especially her. She would never believe me. And she would send me away.

"She may or may not believe me, but I have to remind myself that I'm not a little girl anymore. I'm a grown woman. They can't send me away. But my mind still wrestles with it."

Deanna nodded her understanding.

What if you lose your mom too? What if your kids lose their grandma?

Telling her would be hard and complicated.

" You intended to
harm me, but God
intended it for good
to accomplish what is
now being done, the
saving of many lives."

—Genesis 50:20 NIV

Anthony and I sat in church with the kids between us. He had his arm around them on the pew. As I reached to put my arm around them, my hand landed on his. My index finger rested on a vein. As I pressed gently on the vein, my body got clammy. I wanted to get up and run out of the church, but I froze. The pastor's voice quickly faded into the background. My insides shook as I remembered standing in my bedroom touching him. I pressed on the purple vein with my index finger, thinking it must be spaghetti.

Chapter 15

BOUNDARIES

I heard the gentle whisper in my heart, *Who are you dancing for?*

I knew the question didn't refer to Zumba® or the dance lessons I took as a child. This questioned the dance of life. I learned early on to perform. While it all seemed very staged at times, the costumes and makeup were designed to fit the rhythm needed at the moment. I could wear my Sunday best for church. In the college club scenes, I wore pushup bras and leotard shirts with short shorts. I could transform like a chameleon depending on my environment because it seemed safer to blend in. *Don't stand out. Don't get noticed. Smile, laugh, and pretend you're happy, always.*

I used to do this with little effort, but it did not come easy for me anymore. Rage and anger surfaced, making it harder to be plastic and fake. It became more difficult to laugh behind worry lines and tears. The healing journey exhausted me. My body and mind were worn out from trying to figure out how to appear okay.

At some point, I attempted to stop caring about what other people thought of me. I say *attempted* because the release came gradually. I still worried about people being upset with me. I desperately wanted to be liked, so I tiptoed delicately and tried to find balance with everyone. Then the whisper blew through my heart again like a gentle breeze, *Who are you dancing for?*

We planned a quick weekend trip to PA, and I thought about the question on the long drive. *God, what do you mean? I dance for You, right?*

While we were there, my husband found this charming used-book barn. We spent a few hours inside touring the many twists and turns of books. As I rounded one bend, I spotted a book on the shelf titled *The Divine Dance* by Shannon Kubiak Primicerio. I grabbed it and read the tagline. *If the world is your stage, who are you performing for?* I sat nestled in a corner as I opened the book. The voice again whispered to me, *Dance for Me only. Say yes to Me. Tell them no.*

Who, Lord? Why? And what for?

I thought I already danced for Him only, but He confirmed the message over and over during the next few weeks. At times, the voices in my head and the people in real life tended to drown out His voice. When someone asked me to do something, I quickly responded and said yes. I found it too hard to say no because I feared disappointing others.

He wanted me to say yes to Him by telling everyone else no. Instead of staying so busy, He needed me to be still long enough to hear His voice and move when He said move.

Being still did not fit into my life, but He prepared me for it. I don't like the quiet. I like being busy. I don't like being alone, and I hate saying no. God called me to a place that seemed very quiet and lonely. Yet my life had been so disrupted that I chose to take that route to Him. His love and gentleness wooed me.

You have to rely on My strength now, but wait until there is nothing to do. Wait until My strength is about sleeping, pondering, and engaging with My Word. Wait until you find Me in the quiet. I've always been with you in the hustle and madness. You will taste true peace and experience real joy. Wait until the curtains open. You will twirl on stage to take your bow to a room full of empty chairs. The only clapping you will hear is from Me.

The cadence of His music lulled my heart to be in rhythm with His. He didn't want me to pretend or perform. He wanted me to dance for Him. As I went about my days, it helped to imagine Him sitting front and center in a large, empty auditorium, the sole witness to my heart and actions. No other applause mattered. I wanted to learn to dance for an audience of One. I longed to dance for Jesus.

I shared this with Deanna and talked about the difficulty because I had spent my entire life concerned about what others thought of me. Their opinion of me became my focal point. Between work, serving at church, healing, and being a wife and mom, strings were pulling me everywhere. I needed to let go of some things and be less concerned about what others thought. I took a break from Facebook and quickly realized how much it impacted me. It's so easy to get lost in the sea of social media approval and likes. Social media makes it easy to put out only what you want others to see and know, plus you can filter it up to its shiny best. I knew all too well about projecting the best.

Taking time to be still and listen to His voice led me to the next steps in disclosing the abuse to my mom and brother. I dreaded telling both of them but ultimately decided to tell my brother first.

We planned a trip to Disney with my mom and brother's family. I wanted to go ahead and let them know the truth, but I didn't want to mess up the trip. I certainly didn't want to wait until we were on vacation to bring it up, and it felt wrong to spend that fun time together, then come home and say, "Oh, by the way ..."

I needed to do it, and it needed to be done before the trip. Thankfully, God had prepared me to dance only for Him and say no to others because the voices in my head were the ones I had to fight next. They warned me to stay quiet and that moving forward with my mom and brother would certainly destroy any hopes of having a family. I trembled at the thought but still texted my brother to set up a time to meet.

Incredibly busy with work, he suggested we meet by Facetime, but I insisted we meet in person, even if it meant a delay. He could obviously sense the seriousness in my words, so we arranged to meet halfway at Ruby Tuesday on a Wednesday. I would miss our Wednesday night ladies' Bible study, so I texted them to please pray for me.

Anthony drove. On our way there, I came across the word *Ephphatha* in Mark 7:34 (NIV). In this story, Jesus touched the ears of a deaf man, and said "Ephphatha," which means "be opened." Jesus healed him. His ears were opened. I prayed this word, asking God for my brother's ears to be opened to what I would share with him.

As soon as we pulled in, I could see him anxiously waiting for us along with his wife, Paige. I didn't want to get out of the car, thinking I had made a terrible mistake that would end badly. Anthony assured me we were doing the right thing. As always, he would be right there with me. Then he grinned. "Get out of the car. Let's do this."

I opened my door and got out of the car. As I walked toward my brother, I smiled and went straight into the pretend-all-is-well mode. When we were seated, I immediately grabbed my menu.

Wes looked at me funny and said, "Mik, what is it? Why are we here?"

I kept looking at the menu to avoid his eyes. "Let's order first. Then we'll talk."

The waitress took our order and grabbed the last menu. My brother asked again, "Mik, what is going on?"

I glanced at Anthony and then my brother before staring down at my tightly fisted hands in my lap. I sat quietly for a minute, then looked up. Anthony put his arm around me and said, "Wes, this is hard for her. It may take a minute."

I grabbed my straw and took a long sip of the cold Diet Coke. The soda bubbles were making their way down my throat when the shocking words bubbled out of me. "Wes, Dad sexually abused me."

He sat there stunned with his mouth open. Paige flinched. In obvious shock he said, "No," followed by an expletive. His eyes moved erratically as if searching for an explanation. With genuine concern, he covered his mouth with one hand then asked, "Michelle, how did I not know? I had no idea. I'm so sorry." I started to respond, but he continued. "Does Mom know? Have you told her?"

I sighed. "Honestly, I don't know. I didn't know if you knew. I plan to tell her next."

His next sentence crushed both of us. "Dad was my hero." The words came out and floated around us. The weight of that truth lingered as we sat in silence.

Had he never sexually abused me, he'd be my hero too.

The waitress came and asked if we needed refills. No one responded. Wes leaned forward with his elbows on the table and his chin resting on his folded hands. "Mik, I'm so sorry this happened to you. I had no idea. What can I do for you? How can I help you?"

"Being here right now and believing me is helping me more than you know."

They brought our food. We continued to talk, barely eating our dinner. I told them they could ask whatever they wanted. I would try to answer any questions. We sat at the table for about an hour as I told my story.

When we hugged and said our goodbyes, my brother again said to me, "I believe you and will do anything to help you. Let me know what you need me to do."

Exhausted but still running on adrenaline, my mind raced. On the ride home, the voices in my head shouted that no good would ever come of this. They said, *It's not enough for you to be in pain and be miserable, but you have to go and ruin it for your brother too. Your dad was his hero. Look what you've done.*

My insides twisted, but I also felt the massive weight of lies and deceit lifted from me. I didn't have to lie or pretend anymore around my brother. I texted the friends who were praying for me to thank them for their prayers.

When I woke up the following day, I remained conflicted about sharing the truth. Thankfully, I had a session with Deanna to process it all with her.

Later that afternoon, my brother sent me a beautiful arrangement of flowers. On the card, he thanked me again for telling him my story and said he loved me. Those flowers made me smile and cry at the same time. Plus, they silenced the voices in my head for a bit. My brother knew. It would be okay.

But I still needed to tell my mom.

" The boundary lines have fallen for me in pleasant places; surely I have a delightful inheritance."

—Psalm 16:6 NIV

Sometime during the third grade, I wore a short, white robe and stepped down into the water while holding the preacher's hand. I sat on the bench, with his deep voice loudly proclaiming to baptize me in the name of the Father, the Son, and the Holy Ghost. His soft, white handkerchief covered my nose as he pushed me gently into the water. He brought me back up, and I found my footing. As I stepped out of the baptistry, I looked back to see my dad step in and go underwater. Shortly after we were baptized, he came home from work early one afternoon and told me we needed to take a walk. He held my hand as we walked around the neighborhood and said to me with tears in his eyes, "We should stop doing the things we were doing." I had never seen my dad cry, and I blamed myself for making him sad. I started crying too. "What did I do wrong, Daddy?" But the abuse didn't stop. And now I knew we were doing something wrong.

Chapter 16

ALL THINGS NEW

Our church announced a baptism service. *I should get baptized again*, I told myself. The other voices in my head quickly shouted, *Are you nuts? Who does that? You've already been baptized. You are forty years old. What will people think of you?*

This went on for a few days, but I finally mentioned it out loud to my husband. He liked the idea, so I let my pastor know. My nerves were in a knot as we all walked into church. My husband served as a deacon. We were both in leadership. And now I was getting baptized. I'm sure people had questions, but I desperately wanted to be washed clean.

Even though I didn't think about it often, my previous baptism seemed tainted and dirty. Actually, I tried not to think about it at all.

When my kids asked, I said I wanted to get baptized again because of realizing new things about God in my life. But in reality, I had questions. Could I possibly come up out of the water this time and feel different? Would the deeply ingrained stains in my life be gone? I knew I had been fully forgiven and set free, but would it feel like it this time?

My first baptism hid secrets and fear. This time, the secrets were out, and I didn't feel as scared. I found an old journal from the women's conference I went to with Betty. I purchased the book *A Place of Quiet Rest* by Nancy Leigh

DeMoss. In it she challenged us to do devotions for thirty days. I flipped through my journal and read the daily prayers I wrote for my mom and dad. That's when a vice crushed my heart. How do you pray every day for your abuser? How do you smile and hug him like nothing ever happened? How do you pretend your entire life?

I sat with those questions as my tears stained the ink on the ruffled pages. I knew the answer to those questions, but the little girl inside me needed to hear me say it. "You did it because you had to. You had no choice." Then I added, "And I'm proud of you."

I struggled to get everyone ready for church on time on any given Sunday. I needed extra clothes on the morning of the baptism, so I worked frantically to get it all together.

Once we made it to church, I went to the restroom to leave my change of clothes. I washed my hands, looked in mirror, and smiled at the image staring back at me. Surreal. I wondered if my nerves were mixed with joy.

My knees shook as I climbed the stairs leading to the baptistry. I stepped into the water and took the next step and the next. When the pastor introduced me, I looked to my left and saw everyone in the sanctuary. I couldn't make out their faces, but I knew where everyone sat, so I looked over toward my husband and kids and nervously smiled.

It happened so fast. I heard, "I baptize you now in the name of the Father, the Son, and the Holy Spirit." The soft handkerchief covered my nose as I leaned back onto the pastor's arm and went under the water. My foot slipped as my back arched, but as he pulled me back up, I steadied myself. Someone reached to help me out of the baptistry and handed me a towel.

I looked into the mirror again as I changed clothes and saw myself in a different light. My circumstances had not changed, but something in me changed. The little girl who came out of the water years ago felt dirty. This time I stood taller with my shoulders back and my chin up. My smile stretched so wide you could see the dimple on my left cheek.

I skipped drying my hair because I wanted to get to my husband and kids. I walked into the cold sanctuary with wet hair and rushed for the second row to hug my kids. My husband put his arm around me and squeezed.

They played the same song at the invitation as they did at my first baptism, "Just As I Am." I could hardly move my lips to the words, so moved by this moment of freedom. God gave me a new baptism. With my first one, I remained in complete bondage to my abuser. The newness in Christ that should have washed over me mixed with shame, guilt, and fear.

My first baptism resembled captivity, but this baptism embraced freedom. This time, Christ truly set me free. As my head reached the surface of the water, I breathed in new life in Christ. I left the shame, guilt, and fear of my past in that water. This produced freedom unlike anything I'd ever known.

We went to lunch after church. I took a minute to post the picture of my baptism. I added no caption to explain the significance of the photo, but I knew. And God knew too.

My mom called that afternoon wanting to know, "Why? Why did you get baptized again? You were already baptized."

Her question opened the door to tell her the truth, but I didn't want to take away from the joy. I had no idea how she would respond if I said anything at that moment, and I didn't want to ruin my second baptism, so I quickly ended the call.

A few days later, I decided to tell my mom and asked her to come over after work. When she got there, the kids were on the couch watching a movie. She sat with them for a bit, then I said, "Mom, can you come upstairs with us?"

She glanced at me with a funny expression but followed Anthony and me to our room. I asked her to sit down. She looked over at Anthony and then back at me. "What? What is going on?"

I stood there staring at her, knowing everything would change—for the good or the bad. Life would never be the same for either of us.

She looked at Anthony again. "What is wrong?"

"Brenda, this is difficult for her. Give her a minute. She has to tell you something hard. Something important."

She turned her full attention to me and firmly said, "Michelle, *what* is it?"

"Mom ... Dad sexually abused me."

She looked shocked, then glanced toward Anthony. "He abused me too."

Anthony said, "Brenda, listen to her. This is about *her*. Let her talk."

She turned back to me, and I kept staring at her. Finally, she said, "How did I not know?"

My heart ached—for both of us. "Mom, it's not like he did it in front of you. I had to keep the secret. He said you would never believe me. Plus, I knew you were young when you had me, so I must have been a mistake."

"A mistake? Michelle, you were not a mistake. I chose you. The doctor said I could have an abortion, but I didn't want an abortion. I wanted you. You were *never* a mistake. Why do you think you were? How did I not know? Oh, Michelle, why didn't you tell me?"

"He had me convinced you would never believe me. He would kill himself, or the police would get me and take me away if I told. He said you would put me in an orphanage where terrible things would happen to me. He said no one would ever believe me."

"I would've believed you. You should have told me."

"Mom, I tried."

"What do you mean you tried?" she asked. "When?"

"Do you remember the time you picked me up from my aunt's house after work and I burst into tears once we got into the car? We had watched the after-school special on alcoholism. It scared me. You kept asking, 'Why are you crying?' and I wouldn't answer you."

Mom looked confused.

"Later that night, we were in the car. Dad stopped by the gas station. I waited until he got out of the car before I looked at you and said, 'Mom, if I tell you what made me cry do you promise you won't tell Dad?' You said you wouldn't, so I told you I thought I had become an alcoholic. You said, 'What are you talking about?' and I said, 'Mom, Laurie and I drink wine from the refrigerator at her house. Please don't tell Dad. I don't want to get Laurie in trouble.'"

Mom bit her lip but said nothing.

I hesitated, but Anthony nodded for me to keep going.

"Then the door opened, and Dad got into the car. I sat in the back holding my breath. Before he even got his door closed, you looked at him and said, 'Your daughter thinks she is an alcoholic.' I got in trouble. Laurie got in trouble, and I knew then I would never tell you because you would tell him."

Mom said, "Michelle, I don't remember that. I remember you and Laurie getting into the wine. You could've told me."

"No, Mom, I couldn't. I decided right then and there I could not tell you the secret because too many bad things would happen if I did."

She looked at Anthony and shrugged. "I had no idea." Then she turned back to me. "I'm sorry, but I didn't know. What can I do? How can I help you? What do you need from me? Maybe I need to go to counseling too. What can I do to make up for it?"

"Mom, you don't have to do anything. This is my story, and it's mine to tell. I'm glad you believe me."

"Believe you? Of course, I believe you. Like I said before, he abused me too. That's why I left him," she said.

That night I couldn't sleep. Our youngest made his way into our bed, so I went and climbed onto the bottom bunk of his bed. I lay there staring at the bottom of the bunk above me, my heart full. *Maybe this is what joy feels like?* Giddy, I smiled from head to toe.

All those years, I worried about telling Mom the truth. Finally, my secrets were out. My mom chose me. She wanted me. Best of all, she believed me.

When my friend Lee asked about my baptism, I decided to answer her questions. We became friends when I met Anthony for the first time. She also knew my dad and had seen me interact with him over the years. We decided to meet for dinner at the Cheesecake Factory so we could talk in person.

I don't know what she expected me to say, but certainly not what came out of my mouth. After we ordered our meal, she said, "Okay, tell me about your baptism. Why did you do it?" She sat there grinning with raised eyebrows, awaiting my response.

I paused, took a deep breath, then blurted out, "Lee, this isn't easy to say, and I'm sorry to drop it on you like this, but I have to tell you the truth. My dad sexually abused me as a child. When I got baptized the first time, we were baptized together, so I needed to do it again."

Her visceral reaction became a moment of healing for me. Her smile quickly faded into rage, shock, and tears. I thought we would have to abandon our meals and leave the restaurant. We went slowly. I told her she could ask me anything, and I would try to answer her questions. Eventually, we ate our food. By the end of the conversation, we ordered cheesecake too. She looked angry and wanted justice for me. I didn't know what to make of her response.

I almost regretted telling her because it upset her so much. A part of me appreciated her being furious with him, but another part found it frightening. As we said our goodbyes in the parking lot, I said, "Lee, promise me again you won't say or do anything to him."

She rolled her eyes and said, "Pray I don't pass him in a dark alley." My eyes grew wide, and she quickly assured me, "I'm kidding. I promise I won't say or do anything. Here. I'm unfriending him now on Facebook." She whipped out her phone and pressed the button. Just like that, she deleted him from her life.

If only it could be that simple for me.

I walked into my Thursday session with Deanna sobbing. I could hardly speak at the beginning, but she helped me calm down. She leaned toward me and asked, "What is going on? Are you okay?"

I shook my head and sniffed. "I've had more emotions this week than my entire life put together."

She sighed. "What happened?"

"I feel green again. But this is a new green. A who-do-you-think-you-are kind of green. I'm having a hard time with some friendships at church. It's painful. This is why I don't like to open up to people. When I told my friend Lee, she responded in anger, but then I regretted making her angry. Why do I keep wanting to protect my dad? And my kids. I want to be a better mom, but I'm so afraid of messing up. It's hard for me to listen sometimes. Then I feel guilty because I don't want to hurt anyone's feelings. I'm trying so hard, but it's like I'm being set up. If I open up to deep friendships, I may lose them as a friend. If I step up and connect with my kids, I may screw it all up and make a mistake with them. It's so much safer to keep my distance. To be alone."

Deanna jotted down some notes and then looked up. "Wow, you have really had a week. Let's take this in pieces. Go back to the Cheesecake Factory. Let's start there."

By the end of the session, I understood that some experiences were especially triggering to me right now as I connected them to the fears from long ago.

She summed it up at the end. "You feel especially vulnerable right now. Yes, it is risky to let people in, but it is worth it. Yes, it is scary to be a parent. As you engage and connect more, you are likely to make a mistake or mess up. You may say the wrong thing or hurt their feelings, but your heart is in the right place. Don't let those fears hold you back from going deeper. It is well worth it."

She didn't convince me, but I took in every word.

66 See, the former
things have
taken place, and
new things I declare;
before they spring
into being I announce
them to you."

—Isaiah 42:9 NIV

The little girl in me ... *Stands behind me holding both legs, occasionally peeking around to see. At times, she wants to go back into the dark, sit in the corner. Knees pressed into her chin, hands covering ears tightly, eyes squeezed shut, gently rocking back and forth, mouth sealed. But the breeze on her cheeks brings color to her face causing her to gasp at the freshness. The colorful lights in the sky cause her to strain her neck to see their canvas unveiled. To dance. I feel the loud music beating through her chest. I feel her. I know she's there. I sense her heels digging in, fists clenching at danger, uncertainty, and fear. Facing realities long feared in real time. Eyes wide, anticipating the axis of the earth will soon spin off into orbit. Peeking around, seeing impossibilities become possible. Smelling flowers, picking up rocks, touching mortar along brick walls. Not quite ready to stand beside me and hold my hand. Not quite ready to run ahead. Hair blowing, arms in the air. Looking back. All smiles. Believing all is right with the world.*

THE LITTLE GIRL

Chapter 17

I decided to take a shortcut home after church one day and found myself stopped in traffic. An out-of-shape cyclist with his head down on the handlebars slowly moved up the hill in front of me. He weaved to the left and then the right, probably from sheer exhaustion. Police cars were safely escorting him in the race. Another cyclist rode alongside him and cheered him on. There were also officers directing traffic, so I rolled down my window and asked about the race.

One officer answered, "It's a triathlon."

My mouth dropped, and my eyes widened. Like the cyclist, I often found myself exhausted with my head down on the handlebars of life, feeling inadequate and ill-equipped. I snapped a photo to remember the moment. To remember I'm not alone. This proved to be a beautiful picture of how God will lead me to the finish line. When I think I lack the stamina and endurance to make it, He always brings people alongside to cheer and encourage me. He shields and protects me. I know I can't make it to the finish line alone, but with Him, anything is possible.

How much further is it to the finish line? I wondered.

I considered making my private blog public. I prayed about it, afraid to take the risk. We were reading the story of the ten lepers in my small group. When I read about the one who came back to thank Jesus for healing him, it stood out to me. *I want to be the one.*

173

Sure, I wanted to be the one, but did that mean going public with my blog and telling the world my secrets? The idea terrified me.

A few days later, my youngest came home with artwork from preschool. On a red heart with a bandage on it, he had written, *Jesus healed the ten lepers.* He held it up proudly and said, "Mom, the bandage is there to remind us that Jesus heals."

I briefly considered being the one again and wondered what it would look like for me. I prayed, "God, please make it clear. Should I make my blog public? Yes, no, or wait?"

Later that week, I got my answer when my favorite blogger—Bonnie Gray, the Faith Barista—published a blog post called, "Sometimes, Giving Thanks is a Journey to Become Known." I knew right away. Confirmation. Perfect timing. Again, I closed my eyes and held my breath as I pushed the button to make my blog public. I abruptly closed the computer and walked away.

I began taking better care of myself. I made healthier choices, set boundaries, and paid attention when shame covered me. I confessed my anger for my dad to Deanna. Over the previous weeks, the anger had become intense. Something shifted in me. She could sense it as well. In the beginning, I minimized the abuse by listing all the ways he had been a good father and provider. I rationalized it could have been worse. At least there were no bruises. I sometimes blamed myself by believing his words, "Look what you do to me."

My self-talk changed. I talked to the little girl inside of me now. I wanted her to know the guilt and blame were not hers to carry, and no amount of good parenting erases the devastation of sexual abuse. I needed her to understand sexual abuse is a crime. He committed a crime against her. She did not have to cower in the dark corner of the closet anymore. Still quiet, she listened and engaged. Deanna encouraged me to continue shifting away from judging the little girl and myself by paying attention to my thoughts, words, actions, and even posture.

While cleaning the house with Christmas music playing in the background, the song "Just for Now" by Kelly Clarkson came on. I put it on repeat. As the song played again, my mind raced. When we were out shopping recently, my mom casually asked, "Are you planning to see your dad for Christmas? What about the kids?"

I said, "No." Nothing more.

A few minutes later, she said, "How long do you plan on keeping them from him? You aren't going to let them see their grandpa?"

Everything fired in my mind, but again I answered no. Guilt consumed me, especially about the kids. How would I ever explain it to them? They would occasionally ask about him, and it always made me sad. One of them wrote a note about him at school on Grandparents Day. It broke my heart to read it.

I thought of all the times my mom would say in frustration, "One of these days …" when we were teenagers as if she were planning her own escape and couldn't wait to be free. Did she realize I needed out too?

On our honeymoon, Anthony and I were on a cruise ship for seven days. No one could reach us. I had escaped my dad. I experienced freedom at sea, but then we came back to reality. When we arrived back home, there were still holidays, birthdays, and visits. Add children to the mix. Now there were three more birthday gatherings per year, plus plays and games. At some point after the third child, I deemed escape impossible. I *helicopter-momed* any of the interactions between my dad and my kids and put on my everything-is-fine face. I lived in overdrive, built more walls around myself, and stayed busy to avoid feeling or thinking.

The first Christmas after confronting him confused me. In many ways, it reminded me I had escaped, like being back on the cruise ship again. God gently reminded me of all the times He helped me escape.

One night, not too long before I confronted my dad, he showed up at the house unannounced while I made spaghetti. I went to the door. There he stood, waving. All the alarms screamed inside of me as I smiled and let him in. I walked over to the kitchen counter, picked up my purse and the book about childhood sexual abuse, and took them to my room. I invited him to stay for dinner. As we sat there at the table as a family, the kids did most of the talking. I remained quiet.

I served him dinner that night with a forced smile on my face. I had to turn it on to sit there and function as if life were the same as before. I watched him laugh with the kids and remembered him playing that way with my brother and me at the dinner table when we were kids. That table became home base, a place of refuge. As a child, I laughed and engaged with him at dinner, knowing what would come later.

But I always wondered, *How do you sit in a Norman Rockwell kitchen and engage, then later say and do horrific things to an innocent child in her dark bedroom?*

Suddenly, the weight of not being acknowledged by him at Christmas for the first time in my life hit me. I cried. I didn't cry about the presents. I cried because I wanted him to see me and treat me like a daughter and not a piece of meat. I quickly turned up the music and sang along, which helped most of the sadness dissipate.

Christmas would never be the same, and that would be okay. I had escaped. It had been painful and sad, but also freeing.

I drew a picture of my brain with colored pencils and brought it to my session with Deanna that week. I processed how hard it had been for me to be a *normal* teenager with so many lies and thoughts swirling around in my head. If someone asked about my virginity or if I loved them, those simple questions had very complex meanings in my mind. *Am I a virgin? What is love, really?* These thoughts were tangled with lies and filled me with fear and shame. Seeing all that the little girl inside of me had to struggle with made me sad for her, but also made me proud of her for being resilient. It helped me connect with her and appreciate her innocence.

She made bad decisions too, but her brain had been hardwired to never say no. She coped in ways she understood. She numbed pain. She felt love—or what she thought to be love—when she became physically intimate. Even when she seemed to be at the top of her game, her insides screamed, *You are worthless.* I sat there staring at the image of everything in my brain with tears pouring down my cheeks and thought, *She never had a chance. It could have been so different. What would life look like had the abuse never happened?*

I put my head down and sobbed.

For homework, Deanna suggested I draw something using new coping ways and Scripture to combat all the lies. This exercise created a beautiful image of the work we were doing in therapy. When there are so many lies to untangle, it seems like the work is slow. But every time a lie is unraveled and replaced with truth, there's tremendous healing.

I went home and started on my homework. I made an overlay of my brain and filled it with truth and God's promises to me. Then, on Christmas Eve, the kids and I watched a video about baby Jesus' birth. As the narrator read the Bible story, I heard Luke 1:45 and had to rewind it to listen to it again. "Blessed is she who has believed that the Lord would fulfill His promises to her (NIV)." I ran upstairs to get my Bible so I could find the verse. I underlined and dated it, desperately wanting to believe that God would fulfill His promises to me.

God, help me believe.

We also started a new Christmas tradition. We now stay in our pajamas at home all day and enjoy our time together. It's wonderful.

After Christmas, I shared with Deanna that I thought I should write my story. She said, "Well, what if you wrote your story as if you were encountering Jesus? What if you could insert your story into the Bible? What would that look like?"

I thought about her questions. Then one evening after Zumba®, I sat down and typed away. Instead of writing a Bible story, I wrote it more like a fairy tale for kids. It's about a princess who lives in a castle with her king. A dragon is in charge of watching the gate and keeping the princess safe. But instead of protecting her, he starts waking her up at night and taking her into the deep forest. This changes everything. She doesn't feel like a princess anymore. In the story, the king restores her and helps her heal. I emailed Deanna a copy of it and shared it with some friends. They all encouraged me to keep going.

Maybe it really is time to write my story.

My kids and I cut out snowflakes and decorated them with glitter to hang on our front porch. I wrote this poem about the display as they twirled in the light:

Snowflakes
Each unique
No two alike
Delicate and small in our eyes
Crafted genuine by Christ
Some dented
Broken
Ripped
All glisten
All sparkle
All wonder
When dented meets glisten
And broken meets sparkle
And ripped meets wonder
There is beauty.

Chapter 18

SHINE

We went to the beach for the weekend and had a relaxing time together as a family. On the ride home, I finished the book, *Undaunted*, by Christine Caine and typed this on my phone:

JAN 20, 2014

> After reading Undaunted on the way home, I sense His calling on my life—my purpose. The reason for my being. Formed a clear picture. This is a glimmer.

> My field—my mission as I understand it—is not overseas, not in brothels, or with pimps or trafficking. My field is in churches, where the daughter with the best clothes and finest family suffers horrible abuse at home. Her dad carries the offering plate and sings in the choir. She's hidden. No one has ever told her how wrong it is. For the mom who is trying to balance life and struggles with this deep wound. Right here on Main Street, USA. The silence is deafening. A Sunday dedicated to little girls, pleading with men and women to repent, get help, and preserve children's souls. God help me. It's not a big audience, and not many will follow, but

to the one suffering, it's the brightest light they've ever seen, and it's worth it. One little girl will make the difference. One will matter. Pray for me to walk in obedience with blinders on to distractions.

Impossible made possible, not by me, but by Him alone.

After typing that, I heard:

> You have lost your mind.
>
> But ...
>
> What about ...
>
> I don't know how or what will happen ...
>
> I'm willing to follow.
>
> But it can't be too much. I know the code language. Say it too loud, and even I run. I don't follow certain people because I'm afraid of being associated with loud green. So, it's subtle and code and images of hope that all can relate to online, especially those like me. Stronger in person, but then from a hope and reality perspective. Maybe.

This morning, this verse: For I am full of words, and the Spirit within me compels me. Inside, I am like bottled-up wine, like new wineskins ready to burst. I must speak and find relief. I must open my lips and reply (Job 32:18-20 NIV).

My dreams remained intense. In one, my dad showed up at a bowling alley. I walked away from my group toward him. He made small talk. I said, "What are you doing here?"

"Have you told anyone about what we did?"

I said, "We? How about rephrasing that to say what you did to me? And yes, I have told several people and will tell several more."

"Oh my God. You are going to destroy us. Why would you tell?"

"It destroyed me already, and I want to help others like me because no little girl should be hurt."

He seemed sad about me talking but not about what we did. He kept saying we, and I started getting upset.

"Stop saying we!" I yelled. "You were the adult, me the child!"

Anthony told him to leave us alone, and we went back inside. I lost my purse.

I woke up from those dreams in a panic. Afraid as if I truly had encountered him.

I continued to struggle with relationships and friend-ships, but it helped to process it all in therapy. I told Deanna I wanted to be crazy-brave. "I signed up for She Speaks, and I might write my story. I'm also thinking about sharing at church, but I'm still afraid bad things will happen if I share my whole story."

She leaned in and asked, "What are you afraid will happen?"

I sat there and stared at the corner of the room, tears in my eyes. I finally whispered, "I'm afraid ... he'll kill himself."

I cried on the way back to my office and felt so much guilt. What if he did? I walked in and sat at my desk with the light off. Anthony came in to check on me, then left me alone.

A few minutes later, the door opened. I could hear the conversation.

"Hi, can I help you?" Anthony said.

"Is Michelle here?"

"I'm sorry, she's busy. Is there something I can help you with?"

"No, I will wait."

Anthony came to my door while I pretended to be on the phone and told me I had someone waiting to see me. I quickly dried my eyes and took several deep breaths to regain my composure.

I looked up as the someone made his way in. He stood at my desk in jeans, a white-collared shirt, and a black sweater, holding a CD. When he set the CD on my desk, I saw the words *His Eye Is on the Sparrow* and asked him to take a seat.

He began talking to me about stress. I looked at the CD again and read, *It's Healing Time.* He explained his love for the saxophone and how he created this instrumental disc for others to enjoy and help with stress. His name, Martin L. Herring, and his photo were on the CD's cover.

Considering he came on a Thursday therapy morning, I had to ask him, "Why me? Why did you come here?"

He smiled. "You are my assignment today. I get up each morning and go wherever God leads. Today, he led me to you." As I reached for my checkbook to buy his CD, he looked in his bag and pulled out a journal for me to write in to offer wisdom for his next visitor. He called the journal *Passing the Torch.* He had been collecting notes for over a year.

I took a picture of him holding his CD, then he left. I watched him through the window as he headed to his RV. My husband came up beside me. "What just happened?"

"My angel. God sent him to me today. By the way, I'm going to share my story in church. The pastor asked me to consider sharing on Easter Sunday. I'm going to say yes. It's time." I looked at the CD and read, "It's healing time."

I wrote what I wanted to share on Easter Sunday and made sure to bring my notes with me. As I walked out of the bathroom that morning, one of my friends from college stood in the hallway, visiting for the first time. I hugged her and whispered in her ear to warn her that I would be sharing.

She hugged me back and said she looked forward to hearing me speak.

I sat toward the front and kept glancing behind me, popping my knuckles. There were more visitors than usual on Easter. I saw one of my customers on the back row. Too late to back out now. My hands were shaking so badly, I worried the congregation would see my notes moving as I spoke.

I kept looking at the empty front row and imagining LG sitting there with her bottom lip quivering. Her big brown eyes stared at me with hope because she knew I did this for her. I opened my mouth and let the words pour from my heart, trusting that God wanted me to share my story.

At the end, my heart pounded. My insides shook. Several people came up to me in the foyer and hugged me. A young woman shared her own story with me briefly. An older woman whispered, "Thank you" in my ear when she hugged me. Tears filled her eyes.

I could not wait to tell Deanna I had shared my story. But by the time Thursday rolled around, the focus had shifted to me finding my childhood diary. The dates in the diary confirmed the timeline. Twelve years old. During the cold of winter he removed the orange nightgown and raped me. Twelve years old, like the little girl in Mark 5. They called her dead until Jesus said, "Talitha Koum" or "Little girl, get up!" The little girl in me had gotten up, and I considered her brave.

I had the exciting opportunity to hear Susie Larson speak at a local church in the area. I purchased my ticket and went with a friend to the event. As I backed out of my driveway, I felt prompted to go back and get the CD of me sharing my story at church. It seemed like a ridiculous idea. I knew I might not even see Susie Larson up close at the conference, but I planned to give it to her if I did. As it turned out, I waited in line and handed it to her. It seemed a little awkward, but I tried to trust and obey the still small voice, even when I didn't understand.

Something amazing happened that weekend. At the end of the second day, Susie asked us to write out a prayer and come forward to the altar. I quickly wrote, *Help me to forgive my abusers and those who did not protect me. Hard, especially when they act as if they did nothing wrong.* I stood at the altar and cried as Susie prayed over us. I did not expect to write this prayer request, and seeing it on the page made the emotions heavy and real. Plus, forgiveness seemed impossible.

The following weekend, my husband and I went to Mexico during my birthday and Mother's Day weekend. On our second flight, my husband and I sat in separate sections. I sat by a window. As I opened a book to read, an adorable little girl in a pink, sparkly dress sat down beside me. Her fingers and toes were painted bright pink.

Her dad helped her get settled in with a movie to watch when they announced a delay due to a maintenance issue. After forty-five minutes, we were all hot and getting impatient. The little girl kept changing her mind about what movie to watch and would change the channel. Her dad remained attentive and patient with her. Each time he said, "Okay, sweetheart, let's find *Scooby* again for you. Oh, you want to watch *Frozen* instead? Here you go, sweetheart."

Eventually, the pilot announced we would need to switch planes. I immediately looked for Anthony as a tear rolled down my cheek. Watching the dad interact with his little princess made me sad. It seemed so innocent. I wished that for the little girl inside of me. I missed my kids. I wanted to be patient like that with them.

When we boarded the plane again, I switched seats to be with Anthony. I didn't think I could handle an entire flight with the princess and her doting Father, but I did see them again when we were getting our luggage. I tapped him on the shoulder and said, "You are a good father. Your interaction with your daughter deeply blessed me. You are patient, loving, and kind."

He smiled and said, "Sometimes you have to take a deep breath ... lots of them."

I smiled back and waved goodbye, letting his words sink in.

187

The trip turned out to be wonderful. The hotel, beach, and food were incredible, the time peaceful and restful. Anthony and I enjoyed our time together, but we missed the kids and wished they were with us. When I woke up on my birthday/Mother's Day, my heart ached for my kids. I couldn't wait to get home. I went through some of my mom's old pictures to make a Mother's Day post for her on Facebook.

I can hardly explain what happened next. I found pictures of mom getting married and pregnant with me at fifteen. So young and beautiful. As I typed the words for her post, that small, quiet voice whispered two words in the breeze from our balcony: *Forgive her.*

Honestly, I didn't even know what to forgive at first, but suddenly my heart flooded with compassion for my mom. She chose me. She honored me when a doctor offered to abort me. She had been courageous, and by choosing me, I knew she loved me. I believed it now with all my heart. I grew up thinking myself a burden, but that proved to be a lie. She *chose* me.

When I cried and whispered, "Yes, I forgive her," my entire body flooded with peace and healing. I looked back at the photo I took at the conference when I prayed for help to forgive those who abused me and those who didn't protect me. God answered that prayer. A miracle. Years of lies and negative assumptions ... gone. Many of those lies were tangled in with the abuse. When those thoughts popped into my mind, I whispered in obedience, "I forgive her." My mom made mistakes. So did I. I needed grace, and I needed to give it.

I forgave my mom, but I did not want to forgive my dad.

After our trip, I attended my first writer's conference, She Speaks. My nerves were rattled. When I walked into the first breakout session, I found a seat toward the back.

The girl next to me introduced herself. "Hey, I'm Angela."

I greeted her and told her my name. Then she said, "So, what do you write about?" I froze and stared at her, unable to bring myself to say the words. She raised her eyebrows and waited.

I finally said, "I'm not going to tell you."

Obviously not the response she expected. To change the subject, I mentioned I had an appointment with two agents to pitch my book.

Angela lovingly put her hand on my shoulder and said, "Oh, honey, you are not ready. Let's practice together."

I tried to explain *Journey Pink* to her, but I'm not sure I ever said the words sexual abuse in our initial conversation.

I had my first ten-minute appointment with a man. If trying to explain it to my new friend Angela seemed hard, then talking about it with him seemed incredibly complicated. As I stumbled over my words, he remained gracious, kind, and encouraging.

Thank goodness I had a female for my next appointment. I sat outside preparing and jotting down notes. When I sat across from her, I laid my one-sheet on the table, pushed it toward her, and jumped right into the pitch. By now, I had gotten a bit braver and said the words "childhood sexual abuse" in the first sentence. As I continued, my eyes focused on her three fingers pushing my one-sheet back across the table, screaming rejection. I panicked and started talking faster. She stood up, explaining they were not interested before I could even finish. In shock, I walked out of the room with tears streaming down my face and headed straight for the exit doors. I wondered if others could see a red-inked rejection in all caps stamped on my forehead. I walked through a sea of people as fast as possible to escape.

I sat in my car with the air conditioner blowing cold air on my tears. *God, why am I even here? Why am I doing this? You have the wrong person. I can hardly say the words. This is so hard. This is a waste of time and money.* I called home and FaceTimed my kids, which helped a lot.

"Mommy, why are you crying?" They made me laugh and, eventually, I walked back inside. I saw Angela right away. She made me smile and encouraged me to keep going. She said, "What you are sharing is important, so trust God to make it all happen, in His timing." She also helped me practice my pitch throughout the weekend. She would introduce me to others at an entire table and say, "This is my friend, Michelle. Michelle, go ahead and tell them what you write about." By the end of the weekend, I had shared with several women (thanks to Angela), and they were all very supportive and encouraging. Most were intimidated and scared as well. We all connected.

Christine Caine spoke that year. I looked forward to her message, especially after reading her book, *Undaunted.* I sat utterly energized after hearing her. Her words were like bold, rich coffee. She inspired me to keep going. I had no idea how God would use me, but I wanted to trust Him and obey.

I came home motivated and signed up for another conference. This one would be a blogger retreat at The Cove. I took pages and pages of notes, but there came a moment with Jon Acuff that I will never forget. He talked about being with a large group of teens and having them write down how they saw themselves and why. One of the girls wrote something like, *Touched by a boy at seven. Touched by a man at twelve. Worthless.*

I put my pen down and stopped breathing as he continued. "We were never meant to suffer alone. Your story is a lot of other people's story, and they need you to be brave. Blogging is going first. When you go first, you give others the gift of going second. Go first. Your story matters."

I spent four days away and learned a lot, but those few sentences completely recharged me.

Coincidentally, Jon came and sat at our table at breakfast. He impressed me as personable, kind, and very engaging. Instead of talking about himself, he asked us all to share about our blog. My heart sank. I immediately thought, *Please don't ask me.* I was motivated and recharged but still terrified. I began pumping myself up to say something and could barely pay attention to what others were saying. The person beside me shared. Then someone came to get Jon. I blew out a breath in relief.

Christmas arrived and, with the joy of the season, there were still moments where pain engulfed me. Sometimes the grief, other times the anger. I saw a photo where my dad had given another relative something pink. I experienced complete betrayal and sadness. I did not want to see him, but the daughter in me longed to be cared for and acknowledged in a healthy way.

As I took small, brave steps, my voice got stronger. I started tagging my blog posts with the hashtag #childhoodsexual-abuse. I shared the posts on some of my social media. I hit publish and closed the computer quickly in a panic. The loud voices in my head were getting easier to ignore.

Even my dreams changed. I used to dream of being chased in the stairwell of a dark parking garage with no exits. A new dream included Anthony and light. As we walked around in circles on each level, we would pass my dad as he tried to get my attention. This happened on several floors. I kept ignoring him as he waved frantically at me. Finally, we went around again, but this time, a set of steps led to a bright light. Anthony and I walked up those steps together and walked out into the bright sunshine.

When the new year began, I had learned much about myself. The lies were being replaced with truth, and my incorrect thought patterns were being rerouted. I believed myself to be the apple of God's eye and that He would restore me. Instead of feeling powerless, I started to feel as if I had some power. I engaged and networked with others who were using their own voice. This both inspired me and helped me be brave. I recognized my struggles with boundaries, codependency, and everything being about me. I still had work to do, but I could also see and celebrate my progress. Deanna transitioned me to meeting every other week.

On the way to one of these sessions, "His Eye Is on the Sparrow" came on the radio—the version I love from *Sister Act 2*. I pressed record on my phone at the stoplight and noticed the beautiful pink flags blowing in the wind at the art museum. Toward the end of the song, I gently pressed the gas pedal. That's when it hit me. In a life where I always felt watched, Jesus had been watching me the whole time. *Jesus watches me.* I rushed into Deanna's office, anxious to press play. Tears poured from my eyes as my entire being filled with excitement.

Deanna had a smile on her face and waited for the music to stop. Before she could even ask, I blurted out, "He watches me. He saw it all. When I had to pull up my shirt. When I changed clothes. Took a shower. Used the bathroom or put on makeup. I always felt *watched*. Almost stalked. It never dawned on me that Jesus watched me too. He saw it all. He saw everything I went through. I had another set of eyes in the room. Jesus never took his eyes off me. My witness. Jesus witnessed my pain and shame. He saw it all."

After my session, we went out of town for the weekend as a family, so we missed church on Sunday. Our daughter wanted to have church in the car, so she shared her message called, "God watches us always." I could not help but smile, especially when she added, "Mom, play the 'His Eye Is on the Sparrow' song." Once again, God brought restoration and healing to deep places inside me. He continued to redeem my broken pieces and bring order to my chaos.

With the Bethel music concert only two days away, my excitement grew to hear them sing my favorite song, "You Make Me Brave." Two other friends and I found seats together on one side toward the back of the small venue. As people continued to come, some stood in the aisles without a chair. We were all packed in there together. The music blared loud and electrifying. I could feel every word pound in my chest. Toward the end, they had a time of spontaneous worship and prayer. We sang about the angels singing, the elders bowing down, and about God being worthy. I don't typically raise my hands in worship, but during this song, I stood on my tiptoes with both arms high and straight in the air singing along.

Then it hit me—the memory of being in the oversized red-orange silky gown as a twelve-year-old girl, standing on my tiptoes with both my arms over my head—the worst memory of my abuse.

And yet here I now stood. A forty-year-old woman with both arms lifted high, in safety, to praise and worship my heavenly Father. Instead of being smashed and covered in sweaty yuck and not able to breathe, I stood there open, free, breathing deeply, and wildly covered from head to toe with the cleansing power of His grace and mercy.

Truly clean, from top to bottom. And saturated with His love.

It brought me to my knees. As I dropped to the floor with my head down, I prayed for my dad. I prayed for God to heal him, bless him, and bring restoration to our family. I prayed for God to help me forgive him.

I wanted to forgive my earthly father and let go.

Because I finally felt free and clean in the arms of my heavenly Father.

" The Lord their God will save his people on that day as a shepherd saves his flock. They will sparkle in his land like jewels in a crown."

— Zechariah 9:16. NIV

Shortly after college, I found a church where the preacher talked about the Bible with energy and excitement. I wanted to get my act together and clean up, but I still had struggles. Most Sundays, I sat in the back, hungover and reeking of cigarettes. I always tried to leave before the invitation because a lady named Betty would chase me into the parking lot Sunday after Sunday yelling, "Melissa! Melissa!" One Sunday, she finally caught me. I turned to her and said, "My name is not Melissa. It's Michelle." She apologized and invited me to her Bible study and a beach retreat. I let her finish, turned to get into my car, and said, "I did not come here to make friends." Then I drove away. Betty did not give up on me. If anything, she pursued me even more. I ended up joining them on the beach trip and spent most Friday nights at her house for spaghetti and Bible study. Three years later, Betty directed my wedding when I married Anthony. Today, she calls me the daughter she never had.

Chapter 19

BELOVED

The process of forgiveness had begun but it did not happen easily or quickly. My counseling appointments were still every two weeks, but at times I still struggled with seeing myself as a dirty, bad little girl. How could God allow the harm? More importantly, how could He love me after all I had done and experienced as a child?

A year after the Bethel concert, our church hosted a night of worship. I sat still with my journal in hand and soaked in the music on the back pew.

They had a paint station set up in the foyer, so I decided to paint with watercolors to connect with my inner child, LG. I painted the word *Beloved*. Did I fully believe it? No. The adult part of me thought it to be true, but LG did not. She desperately wanted to know Jesus loved her.

When we went back inside the sanctuary to sit down, Susan Valles stood on the stage singing "How He Loves Us." I loved listening to the Kim Walker-Smith version on YouTube, where she talks in the middle about what it's like to encounter the love of God.

As Susan sang, I imagined LG sitting cradled in my lap. She seemed sad. The adult logic in my brain said, "See, He loves us! He really loves us!" But LG said, "He might love *us*, but He doesn't love *me*."

While sitting in that tension, something shifted. Susan started singing, "Jesus Loves Me," the little kid version. The one I sang when my grandpa took me to church as a little girl. We both knew this song, and we both started singing along. It seemed as if God cradled both of us.

I closed my eyes and cried. For the first time, we both believed He loved us. I could not stop crying, and when Susan came off the stage, I met her in the foyer in tears. LG imagined her being an angel.

I tried to speak, but nothing came out.

Susan smiled and said, "Hi."

Finally, I mumbled, "I can't explain to you what just happened to me."

She put her hands on my shoulders and prayed over me. Such a powerful experience.

We had encountered the love of God together, LG and me. It finally clicked. For the very first time, we could both say at the same time, *Jesus loves me.*

He is a good Father.

His love changes everything. His love changed my life. My prayer is for you to allow His love to change yours.

> I keep asking that the God of our Lord Jesus Christ, the glorious Father, may give you the Spirit of wisdom and revelation, so that you may know Him better. I pray that the eyes of your heart may be enlightened in order that you may know the hope to which He has called you, the riches of His glorious inheritance in His holy people (Ephesians 1:17–18 NIV).

> I pray that out of His glorious riches He may strengthen you with power through His Spirit in

your inner being, so that Christ may dwell in your hearts through faith. And I pray that you, being rooted and established in love, may have power, together with all the Lord's holy people, to grasp how wide and long and high and deep is the love of Christ, and to know this love that surpasses all knowledge—that you may be filled to the measure of all the fullness of God (Ephesians 3:16–19 NIV).

SOME FINAL WORDS ON FORGIVENESS

Shortly after the Bethel concert, I walked into my next counseling session declaring, "I hate my dad. I will *never* forgive him."

And so it goes with forgiveness. For me, it has been a process that ebbs and flows. A new memory or trigger will come up, and I find myself asking God again, "Lord, help me to forgive." In my experience, forgive and forget is more like forgive and remember. As much as I'd love to forget, the trauma inhabits the cells of my body.

When I first hinted publicly about my story, a relative sent me a private message asking for more information and ending with, *The Bible always says to forgive.* After reading it, I felt the singe of hell and never replied to her. Too soon for me to address forgiveness.

My last interaction with my dad occurred ten years ago when I confronted him. Forgiveness does not equal access, especially when you have suffered from trauma. God is still writing my story, and I'm hopeful.

If you asked me today, "Have you truly forgiven your dad?" I would tell you, "Yes, I believe I have forgiven him. I pray for him, and I pray for restoration. I also pray for God to help me continually forgive him—even today. I know I can't do it in my own strength."

My mom and I have maintained a good relationship amid our mutual questions and healing. We have had a lot of conversations and made progress in understanding and supporting each other. She has attended most of the events where I have shared my story and helped me as much as possible. As some memories surfaced, they made me long for her protection and love as a child, leading to another layer of forgiveness. I'm thankful for our restoration.

We are all a work in progress. No parent is perfect.

With all the efforts I put into protecting my children, one of them experienced trauma. The truth is, as parents, we can't always prevent trauma or thwart evil, but we can learn as much as possible about trauma and come alongside our kids with the support to help them overcome. We can validate them, set boundaries, and seek assistance from trauma-informed sources. It is never too late.

Eventually, we shared age-appropriate parts of my story with our kids. My youngest would ask, "Hey, why can't we go to Papa's house?" and I would hear my older children in the back seat whisper, "Shhhh. Don't talk about him. You're going to make Mom cry."

As time passed and they grew older, their questions were more pointed. One day, my oldest child stopped me at the door and said I needed to tell him exactly why he didn't see Papa around anymore. "Mom, what happened? What did he do to you?"

I started with "he hurt me as a little girl," but my son needed more. These conversations led to talks about body safety and assuring my children they could come to us anytime with any information, and they would be believed and protected.

Recently, a new layer of memories surfaced for me along with a medical issue. The wave of healing and forgiveness is building once again, along with counseling sessions. I've learned to trust the work is necessary, and God's timing is perfect. He will get me through it and use it for good.

Years and years of trauma. Layers of trauma. Layers of forgiveness. Messy but all leading to truth and light.

The forgiveness we teach on the playground—"Tell her you're sorry. Okay, say you forgive him"—doesn't play out so well when dealing with trauma, especially with repressed memories. When I first went into counseling, I wanted to forgive and forget and get over it.

Surface memories. Surface healing. Surface forgiving.

My counselor wisely encouraged me to wait and truly process what I needed to forgive, memory by memory. Getting in touch with the pain brought me to a place where forgiveness became complicated yet necessary for my freedom and healing.

How can you heal and forgive what you've locked away?

In Matthew 18:21-22, Peter asked Jesus, "Lord, how many times shall I forgive my brother or sister who sins against me? Up to seven times?" Jesus answered, "I tell you, not seven times, but seventy-seven times" (NIV).

Forgiveness is not always one-and-done. I beat myself up for this because I wanted it to be, but God wanted to heal me, which required remembering. He is gracious, and I only remembered what I needed to heal and forgive. Sometimes forgiveness took longer. Other times, it poured over me like waves at high tide. His grace met me in every memory and every moment.

Healing and forgiveness are delicately interwoven with Jesus at the center, asking, "Do you want to get well?" (John 5:6 NIV).

Take Him with you into your own basement. Sit with Him. Find Him in the rubble with you. Focus on healing. Forgiveness will come. Let Him guide you. He's a good Father.

Healing is worth it, and my prayer is my story will inspire you wherever you are in your own story to say, "Yes, I want to get well." You can be made whole and continue your journey with courage, hope, and freedom in Jesus.

You are never alone. Your King is waiting with open arms.

Then God will come into view,
his arrows flashing like lightning!
Master God will blast his trumpet and set out in a
    whirlwind.
God-of-the-Angel-Armies will protect them—
    all-out war,
The war to end all wars, no holds barred.
Their God will save the day. He'll rescue them.
They'll become like sheep, gentle and soft,
Or like gemstones in a crown, catching all the
    colors of the sun.
Then how they'll shine! shimmer! glow!
the young men robust, the young women lovely!
                              —Zechariah 9:15-17 MSG

One last thing ... I believe you. You are not at fault. Jesus loves you. All the shame holding you back and calling you worthless? It's not your shame. It never belonged to you.

ACKNOWLEDGEMENTS

I began writing *Journey Pink* in 2013. It started as a memoir of my childhood. In 2018, I planned a weekend writing retreat to finish it but started over to write it as a memoir of healing. Jesus has used every word I have ever written to help me heal, and most of the quotes before each chapter are condensed versions of part of the original work. Nothing is ever wasted with Jesus. He has truly made beauty from my ashes. I would not be where I am today without knowing Him as my Savior, Lord, and Father. I pray my journey inspires you to find Him in your story and feel seen, loved, and free.

Thank you to my husband, who has been my greatest cheerleader. Throughout this journey, he has been by my side and never once encouraged me to be silent. He said yes to many writers' conferences, retreats, and time away to write. I sincerely appreciate his love and unwavering support. My kids are the joy of my life and have been a massive part of my healing. Seeing their smiles and hearing their voices encouraged me to continue the journey and take the next step. I love my sweet family with every part of my being.

Thank you to Betty for pursuing me when I wanted to run. Your faithfulness to bring me into your home and pour the love of Jesus into me changed the trajectory of my life. You are an inspiration to me.

Thank you to my counselor, Deanna Towns, who faithfully sat with me in the rubble on Thursday mornings for over three years. Your patience, compassion, and gentleness made me truly feel safe enough to be open and share. Thank you for sitting with me in the tension and heartache when

I struggled and for always pointing me to Jesus. You are a gift and blessing to me.

To my family and friends who have loved and supported me, thank you. To the friend who brought me *The Wounded Heart* in a paper bag to read, I thank God for you. Your courage inspired me to schedule my first counseling appointment, and I'm forever grateful. Thank you to those who listened and made space along the way. I'm thankful for my writer friends who motivated me. Thank you to the friends who poured into me and prayed for me every Thursday at 10:00 a.m. and other times. I pray God richly blesses each of you.

Thank you to my dear and precious friend and first reader, Bernice. She gave me feedback on the entire book before I sent it to the editor. Her handwritten notes and edits will be cherished by me forever.

Lastly, thank you to my editor, Andrea Merrell, for believing in the project and for helping me improve it while maintaining my voice and message. Your wisdom and guidance helped me write stronger and braver.

Thank you to every survivor who has whispered in my ear, "me too." Sharing your story with me gave me the courage to take the next step and make a difference. I pray you will find your voice and do whatever is necessary to heal. Keeping secrets allows the abuse to continue. I know how hard it is to acknowledge. Many may never understand, but I do. I see you, and I support you. Take the time and space you need to find freedom for yourself and the little girl inside of you. Our healing will impact future generations of children who know they are seen, loved, and free.

At last we have freedom, for Christ has set us free! We must always cherish this truth and firmly refuse to go back into the bondage of our past (Ephesians 5:1 TPT).

SOURCES

CHAPTER 1

For more information on Zumba®, go to https://www.zumba.com/en-US.

Susie Larson Blessing: https://www.facebook.com/permalink.php?story_fbid=10150911036218261&id=94958908260

Susie Larson, Blessings for the Evening: Finding Peace in God's Presence, Bethany House Publishers, Bloomington, MN (2013), p. 78

CHAPTER 2

Susie Larson Blessing:
https://www.facebook.com/94958908260/photos/a.135724973260/10151230041458261/

Susie Larson, May His Face Shine Upon You: 90 Biblical Blessings for Mother & Child, Bethany House Publishers, Bloomington, MN (2022), p. 26

Beth Moore Simulcast:
https://blog.lproof.org/2012/09/as-promised-the-great-forsake-and-take.html

Moore, Beth. "As Promised The Great Forsake and Take," The LPM Blog. 15, Sept. 2012, https://blog.lproof.org/2012/09/as-promised-the-great-forsake-and-take.html

Susie Larson Blessing:
https://www.facebook.com/94958908260/photos/a.135724973260/10151170428028261/

Susie Larson, Blessings for the Morning: Prayerful Encouragement to Begin Your Day, Bethany House Publishers, Bloomington, MN (2014) "The New You" p.106

CHAPTER 3

Susie Larson Blessing:
https://www.facebook.com/94958908260/photos/a.135724973260/10151854785943261/

Susie Larson, Blessings for the Evening: Finding Peace in God's Presence, Bethany House Publishers, Bloomington, MN (2013) "Unhurried Days" p. 178.

CHAPTER 4

"Janie's Got a Gun" by Aerosmith:
https://www.youtube.com/watch?v=RqQn2ADZE1A

Aerosmith. "Janie's Got a Gun." Pump. Geffen, 1989.

CHAPTER 5

Susie Larson Blessing:
https://www.facebook.com/94958908260/photos/a.135724973260/10151247804918261/

Susie Larson, Blessings for the Morning: Prayerful Encouragement to Begin Your Day, Bethany House Publishers, Bloomington, MN (2014) "God is Doing a New Thing" p.94.

CHAPTER 6

Just a Little Girl by Amy Studt:
https://www.youtube.com/watch?v=gMevOUPYLZk

Studt, Amy. "Just a Little Girl." False Smiles. Universal, 2002.

"Hungry (Falling on my Knees)" by Kathryn Scott:
https://www.youtube.com/watch?v=erQku5-O0Y0

Scott, Kathryn. "Hungry (Falling on my Knees)," Hungry: Live From London. Vineyard Songs, 1999.

CHAPTER 7

Breaking Free Bible Study by Beth Moore:
https://store.lproof.org/collections/bible-study-in-depth-bible-study/products/breaking-free-member-book-revised-version

Moore, Beth. Breaking Free: The Journey, The Stories (Updated edition). Lifeway Press, 2009.

CHAPTER 8

Cloud, Henry & Townsend, John. Boundaries. Zondervan, 1992.

Boundaries by Dr. Henry Cloud & Dr. John Townsend
https://www.drcloud.com/books/boundaries

CHAPTER 9

"Catch My Breath" by Kelly Clarkson:
https://www.youtube.com/watch?v=HEValZuFYRU

Clarkson, Kelly. "Catch My Breath," Greatest Hits – Chapter One. RCA, 2012.

CHAPTER 10

"Double Dutch Bus" by Frankie Smith:
https://www.youtube.com/watch?v=fK9hK82r-AM

Smith, Frankie. "Double Dutch Bus," Children of Tomorrow. WMOT, 1981.

"Saturate" by Cody Holley:
https://www.youtube.com/watch?v=bKmq6Bd4uLA

Holley, Cody. "Saturate," Earnest Pugh Proudly Presents Gospel's Rising Stars, EPM Music Group, 2014.

CHAPTER 11

I Thought It Was Just Me (But It Isn't) by Brene Brown
https://brenebrown.com/book/i-thought-it-was-just-me/

Brown, Brene. *I Thought It was Just Me (But It Isn't):* Making the Journey from "What Will People Think" to "I am Enough." Avery, 2007.

J Geils Band. "Centerfold" Freeze Frame. EMI America, 1981.

CHAPTER 12

"His Eye Is On The Sparrow" by Lauryn Hill & Tanya Blount
https://www.youtube.com/watch?v=k7Pk5YMkEcg

Blount, Tanya & Hill, Lauryn. "His Eye is on the Sparrow" Sister Act 2: Back In the Habit Soundtrack, Hollywood Records, 1993.

Secrets Simulcast by Beth Moore
https://www.amazon.com/Sacred-Secrets-Living-Proof-Experience/dp/B00NDXGDXY

Moore, Beth. Sacred Secrets: A Living Proof Live Experience (2 DVD's Set). Lifeway, 2014.

Darkness to Light Training
https://www.d2l.org/get-trained/

CHAPTER 13

"Good Feeling" by Flo Rida
https://www.youtube.com/watch?v=3OnnDqH6Wj8

Rida, Flo. "Good Feeling" Wild Ones. Atlantic, 2011.

Daniel Study by Beth Moore
https://store.lproof.org/collections/bible-study-in-depth-bible-study/products/daniel-member-book

Moore, Beth. Daniel – *Bible Study Book: Lives of Integrity, Words of Prophecy.* Lifeway Press, 2006.

"Keep Me" by Patrick Dopson
https://www.youtube.com/watch?v=FZRoJmkGpYc

Dopson, Patrick. "Keep Me," Open The Heavens. OilOnIt Music, 2012.

CHAPTER 14

"Against All Odds" by Phil Collins
https://www.youtube.com/watch?v=wuvtoyVi7vY

Collins, Phil. "Against All Odds (Take a Look at Me Now)." Against All Odds. Atlantic, 1984.

Mom Remembers: A Treasury of Memories for My Child by Judith Levy
https://www.amazon.com/Mom-Remembers-Treasury-Memories-child/dp/1556705948

Levy, Judith. Mom Remembers: A Treasury of Memories for My Child. Harry N. Abrams, 1997.

Clayton King: Healing From Sexual Abuse Sermon at Summit Church
https://summitchurch.com/message/healing-from-sexual-abuse-2-samuel-131-21

Hush by Nicole Braddock Bromley
https://www.iamonevoice.org/product-page/hush-book-autographed

Bromley, Nicole Braddock. Hush: Moving from Silence to Healing After Childhood Sexual Abuse. Moody Publishers, 2007.

"Sad Eyes" by Robert John
https://www.youtube.com/watch?v=l5grdfnGUss

John, Robert. "Sad Eyes." Robert John. EMI America, 1979.

"Radioactive" by Imagine Dragons
https://www.youtube.com/watch?v=ktvTqknDobU

Michelle Viscuse: Lyrical Moments Pinterest Board:
https://www.pinterest.com/michelleviscuse/lyrical-
moments/

"Every Breath You Take" by The Police
https://www.youtube.com/watch?v=OMOGaugKpzs

Sting. (The Police.) Every Breath You Take. Synchronicity.
A&M, 1983.

"Hungry Like The Wolf" by Duran Duran
https://www.youtube.com/watch?v=oJL-lCzEXgI

Duran Duran. "Hungry Like the Wolf" Rio. EMI, Harvest,
Capital, 1982.

"My Songs Know What You Did In The Dark (Light Em Up)"
by Fall Out Boy
https://www.youtube.com/watch?v=oJL-lCzEXgI

Fall Out Boy. "My Songs Know What You Did in the Dark
(Light Em Up)." Save Rock and Roll. Island, 2013.

"Take Me To The King" By Tamela Mann
https://www.youtube.com/watch?v=XvV9p-wU4hk

Mann, Tamela. "Take Me To The King." Best Days. Tillyman
Music Group, 2012.

CHAPTER 15

The Divine Dance by Shannon Kubiak
https://www.beingagirlbooks.com/divinedance.php

Kubiak, Shannon. *The Divine Dance: If the world is your stage, who are you performing for?* Barbour Publishing, 2003.

CHAPTER 16

A Place of Quiet Rest by Nancy Leigh Demoss
https://store.reviveourhearts.com/collections/books-by-nancy-demoss-wolgemuth/products/a-place-of-quiet-rest

Demoss, Nancy Lee. "A Place of Quiet Rest: Finding Intimacy with God Through a Daily Devotional Life" Moody Publishers, 2002.

CHAPTER 17

Sometimes, Giving Thanks Is a Journey To Become Known by Bonnie Gray
https://thebonniegray.com/2013/11/sometimes-giving-thanks-is-a-journey-to-be-known/

blogpost
Gray, Bonnie. "Sometimes, Giving Thanks is a Journey to Become Known" Bonnie Gray, 21 Nov. 2013.

"Just For Now" by Kelly Clarkson
https://www.youtube.com/watch?v=0SSCQ0cweWg

Heap, Imogen (songwriter) Clarkson, Kelly (Singer). "Just for Now" Wrapped in Red. RCA, 2013.

CHAPTER 18

Undaunted by Christine Caine
https://christinecaine.com/content/undaunted-expanded/
gkez8w

Caine, Christine. *Undaunted: Daring to Do What God Calls You to Do*. Zondervan, 2012.

"It's Healing Time" by Martin L. Herring
https://www.amazon.com/Healing-Traditional-Classics-Listening-Herring/dp/B0007NC42M

Herring, Martin L. "It's Healing Time: Traditional Gospel Classics" Audio CD. CD Baby, 2007.

She Speaks Conference
https://shespeaksconference.com/

Go First by Jon Acuff: (this is a tweet similar to what he said at the retreat as a speaker)
https://twitter.com/jonacuff/status/531433957603016704

Acuff, Jon "Go First Tweet" 9 Nov. 2014

"You Make Me Brave" by Amanda Cook
https://www.youtube.com/watch?v=6Hi-VMxT6fc

Cook, Amanda & Bethel Music. "You Make Me Brave" You Make Me Brave Live at the Civic. Bethel Music, 2014.

CHAPTER 19

Susan Valles
http://www.susanvalles.com

"He Loves Us" by Kim Walker-Smith
https://www.youtube.com/watch?v=JoC1ec-lYps

Walker-Smith, Kim. "How He Loves Us" Living with a Fire.
Jesus Culture Music, Sparrow, Capital CMG, 2018.

Susan Valles sings "Jesus Loves Me Medley"
https://www.youtube.com/watch?v=xXgceNsQKqg

ABOUT THE AUTHOR

 **Michelle Viscuse** is a Christian author, coach, speaker, and women's ministry leader. After graduating from the University of North Carolina at Chapel Hill, she owned an insurance agency for twenty-three years. She sold the agency and obtained her MA with high distinction in Pastoral Counseling from Liberty University in the fall of 2021. She also received an Advanced Certificate in Christian Life Coaching from Light University in July 2022. Her short story, "The Garden," was published in the anthology, *Blessings in Disguise with Living Parables* in 2019. She has hosted events, teas, speaking engagements, and Bible studies for women of all ages. She loves to speak in churches because she knows what it is like to sit on the pew and feel desperate for healing truth. Her ultimate goal is to visit as many churches as possible to share how healing from sexual abuse is possible with Jesus and how important it is to have these conversations in church. She founded Journey Pink to help women and teens who have experienced sexual abuse find courage, hope, and freedom in Jesus. She lives in North Carolina with her husband, three children, and a sweet beagle named Maisy Jane. To find out more, please visit her at www.JourneyPink.com.

66 Then you will know the truth, and the truth will set you free."

—John 8:32 NIV

Made in the USA
Columbia, SC
19 May 2023

16603583R00140